CORPORATE PATHFINDERS

A GIFT TO

THE CALIFONIA MARITIME ACADEMY

from

[signature]

MEMBER, PROPELLER CLUB, PORT OF HONOLULU

CORPORATE PATHFINDERS

BUILDING VISION AND VALUES INTO ORGANIZATIONS

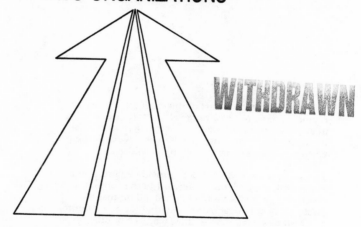

WITHDRAWN

Harold J. Leavitt

DOW JONES-IRWIN
Homewood, Illinois 60430

ISBN 0-87094-695-1

Library of Congress Catalog Card No. 85–61899

Printed in the United States of America

1 2 3 4 5 6 7 8 9 0 BC 3 2 1 0 9 8 7 6

INTRODUCTION

American management has been on a roller coaster ride for the last five years—down, up, and around—and the ride isn't over yet. In the 1960s and 70s that same American management was the flagship of the world's managerial fleet. Remember Servan-Schreiber's *American Challenge*? In that book, published in 1967, the French journalist warned European managers to get on the ball or those supermanagers from the United States would sweep them away. By the early 80s we didn't look like supermanagers anymore.

Whatever the basic reasons, the major immediate catalyst was Japan. The Japanese had landed and were successfully invading Detroit, that most cherished bastion of American manufacturing. Along with automobiles, they moved in on steel, TV sets, watches, and cameras. The American reaction was characteristically swift, if not always sensible. The first rumblings of concern were heard in the mid-1970s. The targets were not managers but MBAs and business schools. Then, beginning about 1980, came a flood of books and media pieces extolling the virtues of Japanese management styles and attacking the newly discovered vices of American management.

In 1980, for example, Hayes and Abernathy published their provocative and widely read *Harvard Business Review* piece, "Managing Our Way to Economic Decline." In 1981 two books in praise of Japanese management, Ouchi's *Theory Z* and Pascale and Athos' *Art of Japanese Management*, did what no other books about management had done in years: they hit and stayed on the *New York Times* best-seller list.

In that first flush of reaction to Japanese successes, some American managers hopped planes to Tokyo and returned laden with those mysterious nostrums of the Orient, quality circles and calisthenics. These were immediately injected into the bottoms of their often unwilling and unready organizations.

The media chorus of criticism of American management grew louder, some of it unbearably loud. The automobile industry is dead and doesn't know it. American management thinks only short term, and besides it's overaged and overpaid. American workers are lazy, uninterested, un-American, and incompetent. American trade unions still think it's the 1940s.

Perhaps the heaviest artillery was (and continues to be) leveled at American business schools. *Time*'s May 4, 1981, cover story was called "The Money Chase," and the lead read "Business school solutions may be part of the U.S. problem." In late 1983 a *Fortune* story headlined "Tough Times for MBAs" talked of the "disenchantment" of many businesses with high-salaried MBAs. In 1983 Tom Peters, by then well known for *In Search of Excellence*, wrote for the *Washington Monthly*, "The business schools . . . are doing more harm than good. I no longer flippantly say, as I used to, close their doors, because now I'm beginning to believe that maybe this idea has serious merit."

After all that beating of breasts and stamping of feet, after that initial search for a quick fix (as quick as a one-minute fix!) and those frustrated blowoffs at managers, educators, unions, and the government, another mood phased itself in. We began to get up off our tails and flex our muscles. We got mad at the Japanese. The Japanese weren't really that good, we told ourselves, and we weren't really that bad. In fact, they were the ones who were really bad. They stole our industrial secrets. They locked us out of their markets while we generously opened ours to them. They were sexists too. And all that bottoms-up participation was really nothing but a disguised application of autocratic and authoritarian power.

The new mood of Japan bashing was coupled with an awakening macho spirit of competitiveness. "Let's beat the bastards." That spirit was beginning to appear as far back as 1981, when Motorola ran a series of full-page ads titled "Meeting Japan's Challenge" in the Sunday *New York Times*. The first of those ads was headlined, "Is Japan's Challenge to American Industry Going Unanswered?" By 1984 the new mood was in full swing. The new set of books and articles about Japan now carried such assertive titles as *The False Promise of the Japanese Miracle*.

One fascinating aspect of all this furor about Japan was how much our view of Japanese management had changed over just a couple of decades. Twenty years earlier Japan had been seen as a faraway, struggling, defeated, copycat nation. In an almost colonialist way, for example, one serious and well-known American scholar had dismissed Japanese management of that period with these words:

There are indications . . . that, by modern standards, today's Japanese management has some shortcomings. Being so sharply differentiated as a class, it fails to communicate effectively with its workers. And in basing entry solely on formal education, it stifles upward mobility from the lower ranks. Its insistence on uniformity and its rigid adherence to age as the principal factor in advancement often lead to stagnation and resistance to fundamentally new concepts. The complete absence of horizontal mobility between firms tends to divide the managerial class into airtight compartments. Although Japanese management has been quick to borrow new techniques of production, it has not been so successful in the field of merchandising. For example, it lags be-hind its German and American competitors in exploring and developing foreign markets for its manufactured products, despite the fact that its very survival depends upon the expansion of its foreign trade. And as we have indicated, it has been slow to make innovations in general management comparable to those being introduced in most other advanced countries.[1]

Note that what American eyes then saw as managerial weaknesses are the very things we now try to imitate, holding them to be the sources of Japanese managerial strength.

We finally began, in 1983 or so, to get over our obsession with the Japanese. A wave of more positive thinking set in. Optimistic and reassuring books and articles appeared. Most American managers had just been misled and misguided, the new literature said, seduced from the path of virtue by those damn MBAs and staff types. The very best of American managers hadn't been taken in, though; so if we looked at how the good ones did it, the rest of us could soon get back on track. Peters and Waterman's optimistic *In Search of Excellence* was received by senior American managers like manna from heaven. It sold at a level never before even imagined for a book about management. It urged a return to simplicity—to the straightforward man-to-man, hands-on, American way of doing things. CEOs ought to fire their staffs, get their butts out of their hushed top-floor offices, and wander out onto the shop floor. Real managers get out there and lead the troops. Evangelists, not number crunchers, are what American industry needs!

But by this writing (in late 1985), even that recipe has begun to lose its appeal. Those ideas about obsessive and dedicated personal leadership, we are now told, may sell a few chickens, but they won't run a railroad. It's all drivel and balderdash. *Business Week* says "Oops" on its cover of November 5, 1984, arguing that some of that kind of excellence doesn't look so excellent even three years later.

No, American management is not off the roller coaster yet. But the ride we've taken has had its good points. Along with all the noisy overreaction, some very positive rethinking has gone on. Years earlier, after the Russians launched the first sputnik, Americans had put themselves through the same sort of frustrated self-flagellation. But that wasn't just a tantrum either. It was also an introspective reassessment of American education, a reevaluation and a partial renewal. The sputnik of Japanese management has catalyzed a serious reassessment too, though the process still has a long way to go. Some of my European friends dismiss all the hullabaloo of the last few years, treating it as typical American sound and fury, signifying nothing. I think they're wrong. It's the Europeans who have underreacted, behaving as though the world were really standing still.

While the Japanese have been an important catalyst, they were not the sole cause of American management's current problems. The problems went deeper. They would have shown up anyway, though perhaps more slowly. Our managerial history and our beliefs about good and bad managerial thinking were certainly causal factors too. From about 1900 onward we began to equate good managing with tight controls, steep hierarchies, and formalized organizations. While that kind of structure made sense for its day, it turned out to be a hard house to remodel as times changed. Some of the noise of the last few years is the sound of efforts to modernize that old house. Since we're still trying to do it on the old foundation, the job will be expensive.

Some of the noise is also the creaking and squeaking that accompanies change in our thinking processes. We've become so skillful at analytic thinking, and so busy exploiting its huge potential, that we've let our imaginations get rusty. Now we're trying to get those old creative engines humming again.

The noise is dying down a little, and some of the places where we need changes in structure and in thought have become easier to identify. Some significant rebalancing of American managerial priorities certainly seems to be in order. This book tries to focus on a few places where that need for rebalancing is greatest. Its approach reflects a convergence of three trains of thought. The first is thought about the nature of the present unsettled state of American management and American management education. The second is thought about thought itself. I have had a long-standing interest in thinking styles—in the ways people use their heads and in the ways members of different occupations and professions think about the same problems. The third is historical thought. American managerial history is not only fascinating; it is also enlightening. How have current management beliefs and attitudes gotten here from there? How much has our history filtered our vision? Are contemporary managers, most of whom show little interest in their profession's history, nevertheless its unwitting intellectual prisoners?

This book, a product of those three diverse trains of thought, proposes some ways in which we might usefully modify our perspective on the functions of the contemporary executive. The proposals are neither particularly original nor very radical. While they are consistent with the general direction of recent calls for more personal leadership, clearer and simpler missions, and better-managed corporate cultures, they try to take a balanced perspective. The key ideas are hung on a simple model of managing that treats the managing process as an integration of three broad phases, which I call *pathfinding, problem solving,* and *implementing.*

The book does not deal much with "macro" issues. It is not about industrial policy, or antitrust legislation, or Japan, Inc. It sticks to the internal, in-house aspects of managing the organization—to the relationship between the beliefs, attitudes, and practices of managers and the ways in which organizations change and develop.

One last point. Despite the tone of some of this introduction, this is an optimistic book. American managers are coming back fast. The traditional American capacity for rapid self-modification is showing itself once more. Even American business schools are moving. At a barely perceptible snail's pace they too are swinging their academic bulk into the winds of change.

Note

[1] The quotation is from F. Harbison, "Management in Japan," a chapter in *Management in the Industrial World*, ed. F. Harbison and C. A. Myers (New York: McGraw-Hill, 1959), pp. 263–64.

ACKNOWLEDGMENTS

My debts are extensive. So many people have contributed directly and indirectly to this book that I cannot possibly name even most of them. So herewith a blanket thank-you to all students of all ages in all courses and programs in which I have taught and learned, to colleagues at Stanford and elsewhere, and to those managers in the United States and abroad with whom I have been privileged to work and think.

Over the last two years, an entirely informal group, which came to be called the Bach Chamber Society, has stimulated and challenged my thinking about many of the issues raised in this book. I am grateful to all of the participants in that group, especially to Lee Bach, Gene Webb, Chuck Holloway, Homa Bahrami, and Al Hastorf.

My special thanks to Ms. Ann Margulies, who edited, organized, and advised with skill and compassion; and to Mrs. Arleen Danielson, who, with unbelievable patience, converted the manuscript from my hieroglyphics to the typewritten page.

H.J.L.

CONTENTS

CHAPTER 3
Pathfinders and Pathfinding: Vision, Values, and
Determination, **47**

One problem: Three ways of looking at it. Styles of thinking: Pathfinders and problem solvers aren't usually on the
same wavelength. Three pieces of pathfinding: Vision,
values, and determination. Vision. Values and pathfinding. Determination. Characteristics of pathfinders and
pathfinding: A reprise.

CHAPTER 4
Pathfinders: Can We Develop Them, or Must We
Wait for God to Deliver Them? **77**

A step toward teaching vision: Teaching creativity and
imaginativeness. Teaching creativity: Some possibilities.
Clarifying values. Fostering determination. Developing the
whole pathfinding pattern.

CHAPTER 5
On Becoming a Pathfinder: Can We Help
Ourselves? **101**

Personal pathfinding: Breaking out. Enhancing creativity.
Creative problem finding. Creative problem making.
Values. Determination. Once again, can pathfinding be
self-taught?

CHAPTER 6
Pathfinders Inside the Organization: Is There
Room at the Inn? **121**

CHAPTER 7
Building Pathfinding into the Organization: Small Steps toward Large Changes, 141

Why is it so exciting to be young? Must older organizations lose their #1 yeast? Some #2-type advice on building a #1 climate into the large organization.

CHAPTER 8
From Organizational Mission to Organizational Culture: Managing the Mist, 163

Organizational culture: Is it for real? And if it is, does it really matter? Changing old cultures: Can managers move mountains? Culture building: A #1–#3 combination. Socialization: The cultural production line.

CHAPTER 9
Building Pathfinding Cultures: Toward Plural and Parallel Pathfinding, 187

Pathfinding leaders and pathfinding cultures: Does A cause B? Parallel and plural pathfinding cultures. The role of small groups in pathfinding organizations. Maintaining a pathfinding culture. A reminder: Pathfinding cultures are risky.

CHAPTER 10
Keeping the Whole Act Together: Pathfinding Is Only One Part of the Managing Process, 209

Getting here from there: The long 1–2–3 horse race. The end of the 2–3 model of management education: Managing requires more than just a sharp mind and a silver tongue. Toward a managerial trinity: Fitting #1 back into the managing process. A final caveat.

PATHFINDING, PROBLEM SOLVING, AND IMPLEMENTING:
The Management Mix

Every couple of decades managers and academics scratch their heads and once again ponder some tough old questions like these: What is managing *really* all about? What are managers doing right? What are they doing wrong? What should they *really* be trying to do?

Even though such questions will never be finally answered, they are healthy, indicative of a recurrent readiness to change and to experiment. This time around, they seem especially important, driven partly by anxiety and uncertainty about what it will take to cope with the volatile, complex, and fast-changing world that lies ahead.

This small book tries to focus more clearly on questions of this kind, and to suggest partial and temporary answers to some of them. It begins with a simple three-part description of what the managing process looks like in the late 1980s. Those three parts then serve as handles for examining where American management has gone right and gone wrong in recent years, and what kinds of corrections and changes seem to be in order.

The book's general argument is that we have unintentionally neglected the visionary, pathfinding part of the managing process over the last 20 years. We have, at our peril, put most of our energies into two other areas—into planful, analytic, systematic methods of problem solving and into the action and people-oriented implementing parts of managing. Only since the early 1980s have the bills from that neglect of pathfinding become obvious. We are right now in a healthy but hectic period of repayment, regrouping, and renewal.

This first chapter outlines the three-part model of the managing process and briefly describes each of the three parts. The main purpose of the chapter is to lay the groundwork for understanding why the neglect of pathfinding by managers and educators alike has come close to costing us our managerial shirts.

The three parts into which this model divides managing are these: #1 pathfinding, #2 problem solving, and #3 implementing.

Consider them in reverse order, starting with #3 *implementing*, because that one is such a pervasive element of our image of the modern manager. For here lies the macho mover-and-shaker part of the managing process, as well as the office politics and manipulative parts, and even the participative, human relations parts. It is this implementing side of managing that shows up most often in soap opera managers and in movie versions of the manager. Implementing is about *action*, about getting things done through people, making things happen. Implementing is getting the bricks laid, the services rendered, and the product delivered. Implementing is *doing* things *through others*. Managers are people who get things done. They persuade, cajole, influence, command.

But managing is not just about implementing. It is also about *problem solving*. Managers have to organize, plan, and make decisions. Good managing takes some IQ points as well as some capacity to get things done. Managing means taking hold of complex, messy, ill-defined problems and converting them into organized, systematized forms. Managers have to make rational decisions about products, people, and markets; they have to allocate scarce resources sensibly. Managers must be thinkers as well as doers. They have to make order out of chaos.

Behind both the problem solving and implementing parts of managing, there lurks still another part of the process, the much fuzzier, less observable #1 part, here called *pathfinding*. Pathfinding is the major focus of this book, and while ephemeral and hard to measure, it is an incontrovertibly real and critical part of the managing process.

#1 pathfinding is about getting the right questions rather than the right answers. It is about making problems rather than solving them. It is *not* about figuring out the best way to get there from here, nor even about making sure that we get there. It is rather about pointing to where we ought to try to go.

#1 pathfinding, that is, is about mission, purpose, and vision. #2 problem solving is about analysis, planning, and reasoning; and #3 implementing is about doing, changing, and influencing. Our model of managing is about those three critical sets of activities and about the back-and-forth interactions among the three.

The model can be pictured this way:

A Model of the Managing Process

#1	#2	#3
Pathfinding	Problem solving	Implementing

The wavy vertical lines are there to show that the boundaries between the pieces are often foggy, and to suggest that movement from any one to any other can be both difficult and critical. It is not enough, that is, for the manager to be competent in one of these three, or even in all three at once. The manager had also better be skillful at moving across the harsh terrain that often separates them.

That three-part view of managing can (and will) be applied at several levels. For the individual manager, the three parts can be treated as three styles of managing. Some managers, that is, use predominantly pathfinding styles; others are problem solvers; still others are implementers. Most of us mix the three styles, presumably to fit appropriate situations. But are we really that flexible? Can we learn new styles late in life? How? Aren't the three parts of managing mutually contradictory?

At that same individual level, educational questions arise. In the education of managers, should we try to teach a blend of all three and shoot for "balanced excellence"? Have business schools taught any pathfinding at all? Could they? Or should they try? Later chapters examine such questions from an individual perspective.

The three parts—pathfinding, problem solving, and implementing—can also be looked at from an organizational perspective. Do organizations need pathfinding individuals? In what proportions? At the top? Throughout the organization? Should the three parts of the process be specialized, with each the responsibility of a particular group or level? Should we let R&D, for example, do the pathfinding, while engineering does the problem solving and sales does the implementing? Or should the CEO be the pathfinder, with the staff people the problem solvers and all the rest the implementers?

Do large ongoing organizations need more pathfinding types? Won't that erode discipline and lead to anarchy? How can the individualistic, high-risk pathfinding style be integrated into the participative kind of implementation that has grown so prevalent in recent years?

This three-part model can be considered at a societal level as well. To what extent is pathfinding part of the heritage of most Western nations? Has some of that heritage been lost? Have recent educational policies and practices encouraged or suppressed pathfinding tendencies? Has the growth of very large organizations discouraged individualistic pathfinding? Do the cultures of most organizations, especially large and old ones, need a good shot of pathfinding style—a mood of urgency, a push toward innovation, a salient sense of mission?

Implementing

Let's add a little meat to these bones by looking at each part of that three-part model in more depth. Again we start at the #3 end.

Implementing is not done by managers alone. Each of us implements all the time, whether or not we wear managerial hats. We mow the lawn, drive the car, fix the lamp, cook the dinner. But when implementing is part of the managing process, it has a couple of attributes that distinguish it from implementing in nonmanagerial settings.

First, managerial implementing is always done through other people. That's of course not at all a new idea. My old mentor Douglas McGregor used to define all of managing that way: "Managing is getting things done through people." While in other parts of life we can often implement our own decisions, managing human organizations invariably requires convincing other people to mow our lawns and cook our dinners. Implementing in organizations almost always requires the manager to persuade or command or manipulate or force other people to change their present behavior, to do what the manager wants done instead of what those people are now doing. *Managerial implementing is therefore a highly social activity.*

Second, managerial implementing involves changing other people's behavior, and therefore *it is a highly emotional activity.* Everything the social sciences know about changing behavior says that people change for emotional reasons far more than for rational reasons. It's love, hate, greed, loyalty, jealousy, and passion, much more than cool, pure reason, that drive us to change our ways. So the implementing part of managing has more to do with people's hearts than with their brains. It is not through logic and rationality that we persuade our employees to improve quality or increase productivity. It is through pride or ambition or loyalty. Getting people to do what you want them to do is much more a gutsy than an intellectual process.

But what's new? Hasn't that always been the case? Yes, but in our new world of knowledge and information, the role of emotionality has, paradoxically, gotten bigger, not smaller. In the old world of mostly physical arm-and-leg work, and in the social environment of those days, implementing was mostly focused on the fear-provoking emotionality of command and control or on the emotionality of paternalistic protectionism. In today's more professional, more

educated, and more egalitarian organizational world, implementing becomes an issue of persuasion, negotiation, and
inspiration rather than of command or protection.

Skill in working with human emotionality is not only
rare in managers; it is often seen as "unmanagerial." Recent
generations of young managers have, in general, been
taught to use their heads much more than their hearts. They
are supposed to learn to be rational, objective, hardheaded,
professional. But when managers try to influence emotional
human beings with exclusively rational tools, trouble starts.

Where and how, then, does one learn implementing
skills? Imagine a teenager asking you something like that. "I
really like that implementing stuff. I'd love to learn how to
win friends and influence people. But how do I learn to
become a great implementer? What should I study? What
occupation should I try?"

It is not very difficult to identify some occupations in
which implementing skills are critical to effective performance. How about direct selling? Or line supervision in a
manufacturing plant? Surely platoon leaders in the Marine
Corps had also better learn to be pretty good at implementing. They are helped along, of course, by rank, military
structure, and all the rest, but in the last analysis it's the
platoon leader who has to get those 50 marines to take
that hill.

Litigating lawyers had better understand emotional implementing too. They have to persuade judges and jurors, to
cajole and browbeat and sweet-talk witnesses. The litigators
I have encountered in American law firms are killers, competitors. They are often singled out by other lawyers as a
special subgenus of the legal species. Litigators worry about
whether to select younger women for this jury or whether
they would be better off with older men. They focus on the
idiosyncrasies and characteristics of the opposing lawyers
and on those of the judge. They work on people's prejudices
and impulses, just as a very good salesperson does.

The band of occupations that can offer a young person practice in implementing is very broad indeed. It includes not only second lieutenants, lobbyists, and salespeople but also psychiatrists, counselors, organizational development people, and others in the "helping professions." Whether they acknowledge it or not, the members of these professions too try to change people's behavior by largely emotional means.

So what may seem like a collection of very strange bedfellows fits into this implementing part of the world of managing. Two bonds tie them all together. First, in all the varied kinds of managerial implementing, *human emotionality is the essence* from which change is made.

Second, most members of these implementing occupations think *small*. They think about people singly or in small numbers. For most skilled managerial implementers, human beings are *real*. They have names, faces, personalities, individual idiosyncrasies. They are not masses or statistics or hired hands, as they often are for extreme #2 problem solvers. So it should come as no surprise that when #3 implementers try to design large organizations, they usually want to use small groups as their building blocks, piling up pyramids composed of many small human units.

Problem solving

Let's turn now for a closer look at the #2 problem solving piece of the managing process. If the key word for #3 implementing is *action,* then the key word for #2 problem solving is *analysis.* Problem solving (at least as we in the Western world see it) is about reason and logic. It is about orderly, systematic approaches to problems. It is about planning and coordinating.

We know a good deal about how to teach problem solving skills, much more than we know about how to teach implementing skills. Indeed, that's what most education is all about. Reading, writing, and arithmetic are all analytic problem solving skills. A caricature of the complete #2 problem solver does not look at all like the fast-moving, fast-talking caricature of the implementer. The problem solver casts an intellectually reserved shadow. The image is of the steel-trap mind poring over the printout by lamplight, figuring out the right answer, the logical solution, the defensible decision, the optimal strategy.

If that inquiring teenager likes the #2 problem solving image and asks you where a young person ought to go for training to become a great problem solver, the answer should be quite easy. One good place to go is the Modern American Business School. Something like 80 percent of the contemporary MBA curriculum has been focused on the #2 analytic problem solving part of managing. That's the place to learn about linear programming, systems analysis, operations research, and econometric methods, about how to build marketing models and how to do financial analyses. Look at the catalog of any MBA school. The course titles use the word *analysis* again and again: Financial Analysis, Market Analysis, Decision Analysis, Economic Analysis. Go to business school to learn to program what has previously been unprogrammable.

But business school is only one of the places where the young person can learn how to do analytic problem solving. He or she might also try engineering or accounting or management consulting or tax law. All of those professions require high levels of analytic skills. They require logic, consistency, and orderliness. While it's likely that members of those professions are sometimes talented in other ways too, analytic skill remains a sine qua non for competence in all of them.

Given all of that emphasis on analysis and logic, it is no surprise that all-out #2 types take a dim view of emotionality. While for #3 implementers emotionality is the raw material of change, for orthodox #2s that same emotionality is likely to be seen as noise in the system, as a sign of human imperfection. In a few million years the full rationality that God so clearly intended will evolve. Real men aren't emotional. So one of the trouble spots in the managing process is located at the junction of #2 and #3, where rational problem solvers meet emotional implementers.

Notice too that analytic occupations carry very high status in Western society, in contrast to the somewhat lower status usually ascribed to many of the implementing occupations, such as selling or manufacturing management. It's OK for your son or daughter to enter any one of them. And they pay well too. Among MBA students, for example, it has been the jobs in consulting and financial analysis that have been viewed as the most desirable ones, at least until recently. Selling has been viewed as low class, and manufacturing as too dirty.

A caveat: While much of the problem solving part of managing can be learned through quantitative, analytic training, not *all* of it can be picked up that easily. There is, as every manager knows, more to real-world problem solving than can be found in the problem sets at the end of the chapters in the accounting text. There is more uncertainty in the real world, more unforeseeable variability. So such words as *judgment, experience, wisdom,* and *good sense* have stayed on our recruiting checklists, even as #2-type academics seek ways of making them unnecessary.

Pathfinding

If implementing includes large emotional components and if problem solving includes large rational and analytic components, how can one characterize the #1 pathfinding part of the managing process? The central issue of pathfinding is not influence or persuasion, nor is it reasoning or systematic analysis. The key word here is *mission*. The pathfinding part of managing is the homeland of the visionary, the dreamer, the innovator, the creator, the entrepreneur, and the charismatic leader. The central questions are very difficult and often unaddressed: How do I decide what I want to be when I grow up? What should this organization try to become if it could become anything imaginable? What do we really want to do with this company?

The #1 pathfinding world is highly personal and subjective, with answers, where there are any, emerging more from within the self than from a diagnosis of what's out there. Pathfinding is the ephemeral part of managing that deals with values, aesthetics, and beliefs. Putting faith before evidence, pathfinders often violate #2 problem solving precepts. But they also build new worlds.

Do we even need such soft, subjective stuff to manage the modern organization? The answer is unequivocally yes, whether we derive it from social or political or organizational observation. The pathfinding role has always been a critical driving force in the rise of human institutions. From the founding of the United States to the development of IBM to the birth pangs of that new little start-up company, the beliefs and visions of a few stubborn souls have always driven innovation and development.

By far the best illustration of a pathfinding statement that I can offer is familiar to all Americans. It is the second sentence of the American Declaration of Independence: "We hold these truths to be self-evident, that all men are created equal, that they are endowed by their Creator with certain unalienable Rights, that among these are Life, Liberty and the pursuit of Happiness."

What an assertive, pathfinding declaration that is! It must have driven the #2 problem solvers of the day absolutely wild. All men are created equal? How do you know? What's the genetic evidence? "Rights" like "Liberty" or "the pursuit of Happiness"? How do you measure such stuff? "Self-evident" truths? No evidence required? No data to support them? And could anyone, even armed with the most clear and potent evidence, have changed those Founding Fathers' minds? They weren't to be distracted by mere facts!

The pathfinders whom most of us would cite as memorable are also necessarily skillful as implementers. We only remember them if other people have joined up with their visions. Visionaries who do *not* influence others to follow them are simply forgotten. Or if they are remembered at all, they are remembered as impractical dreamers, not as men and women of vision. Indeed, that almost defines a *charismatic leader*: A charismatic leader is a #1 pathfinder who is also successful at #3 implementing—someone with a sense of mission who can also get others to join in.

Pathfinders need not be heroes. They are not always lovable or even smart. People with unusual ideas, strong commitments, and deep beliefs may also be intransigent, single-minded, unforgiving, or simply stupid. It's not just the good guys, the Jesus Christs and Martin Luther Kings, who qualify as pathfinders. Some great pathfinders were more than a bit unpleasant; some were very bad fellows. Adolf Hitler belongs in that set, as does Jim Jones of Jonestown in Guyana, and probably so too do many of the robber barons of European and American industrial history.

In business, the pathfinders are easiest to spot among entrepreneurs and founders of companies. Watson of IBM, Hewlett and Packard, Land of Polaroid, and Freddie Laker were all people dedicated to building their dreams into realities. Such pathfinders are not always pleasant or friendly, and they may not be successful in the long run, but they are all stubborn, committed believers with strong, clear notions of good and bad.

Pathfinders also turn up in old established companies, but less frequently. When they do, they inject new mission and purpose into old organizations. In the early 1980s Lee Iacocca, for example, may have done just that at Chrysler, and Carlson at SAS. In both cases they have turned around their companies' spirits as well as their P&Ls.

To what education and which professions, then, should we direct young people who decide that pathfinding is what excites them?

It's much harder to answer that question for #1 path-finding than it was for #2 problem solving or #3 implement-ing. Pathfinders seem far easier to identify than to develop. Perhaps we should point young people in directions quite unrelated to the contemporary management scene. We could suggest that they seek their fortunes among artists and architects, or among philosophers and religionists, or among theoretical physicists; or perhaps we should recommend a broad liberal education, if such a thing still exists.

Indeed, one can argue that management education as we now practice it would do very little to enhance pathfind-ing abilities. Our methods of educating and developing new managers have not only neglected pathfinding; they have often downright clobbered it. While problem solvers and implementers, whether in companies or in universities, fight like the devil with one another, they also share a common interest (sometimes unconscious) in keeping the pathfinders out.

For obvious reasons, #2 problem solvers don't want stubborn, intractable, impractical visionaries around. Path-finders can seldom offer (and seldom care to offer) hard evidence for their choices; and hard evidence is the essence of modern problem solving. Pathfinders often ignore the rules, or act impulsively, or wave off what they see as trivial details.

Here in northern California's Silicon Valley one version of the clash between #1 and #2 styles has occurred several times in recent years. It happens as small companies succeed and grow larger. At some point, the venture capitalists or other investors convince the #1-type founders that their now chaotic organization needs discipline and control. So a #2-type COO is brought aboard. Occasionally the marriage works, but frequently the freewheeling #1 style of the founder is just too disruptive for the control-oriented #2 manager (or vice versa), so sparks fly, heads roll, and energy is diverted from the main target just when it is needed most.

#3 implementers are also likely to feel cool toward those unmalleable, individualistic pathfinders. Contemporary #3 types are particularly oriented toward teamwork, consensus, and cooperation among an organization's members. No matter how positively we may value such styles, they do not fit neatly with the stubborn, determined individualism of pathfinders. #1 pathfinders often become team leaders, but they are seldom good team players.

Outstanding pathfinders, problem solvers, and implementers: Some examples

Occasionally rare and unique personalities turn up who leave their mark in history almost entirely as implementers, or problem solvers, or pathfinders. They are so good at that one part of managing that it completely overshadows the other two. It's worth identifying a few such extraordinary people, people known to almost all of us, to help draw a clearer picture of the differences among the three parts.

Who, for example, among great public figures familiar to all of us, is the implementer par excellence? Who is preeminent among the problem solvers? Who are the outstanding pathfinders?

Certainly one ideal nominee for an Oscar among implementers would be Lyndon Baines Johnson, at least that part of him that keeps coming through in his biographies. Implementing can be done in many ways, and Johnson's was only one way. He was so good at it, however, and it was so central to his managing style that he serves as an excellent example.

As president, Johnson was certainly not considered by most observers to have been a particularly great #2 intellect, nor a great planner or organizer. Neither was he regarded as a great #1 visionary pathfinder. He did, the reader will remember, try to establish a mission for America, his Great Society, but that notion somehow never took hold, perhaps because many Americans weren't sure he really believed in it himself.

But Johnson will always be remembered as a top-notch implementer. His skill at twisting the arms and stroking the egos of congressmen was legendary. He could shuffle greed, love, fear, and sentimentality to get what he wanted. He could make compromises, negotiate workable solutions. He could get it done. In one sense, he was a very good planner too. He did his homework before taking on the people he wanted to influence. He learned all about their children and their lovers and their hobbies and their hangups. And he used whatever tactics were needed to do the job. He got things implemented through people.

The stories left behind from the Johnson presidency reflect those characteristics. Johnson's memorable quotations were invariably pragmatic and earthy. One of his favorites: "Don't spit in the soup; we all have to eat."

On one occasion, the story goes, an aide came to him to ask, "Mr. President, why are you climbing into bed with Joe Smith, who has always been your enemy? For years that guy has been trying to destroy you, and now you seem to be forming an alliance with him." Johnson is said to have replied, "I'd rather have him inside the tent pissing out than outside pissing in."

No statesmanlike rhetoric here. Those Johnsonisms are not likely to make *The World's Great Quotations*, but they catch Johnson's pragmatic emphasis on doing what one has to do to get the damn job done. And they surely also illustrate his awareness of the relevance of human emotionality in the implementing process. Typical of the approach of excellent implementers, these quotations illustrate two key characteristics of #3 skill—attention to emotionality and attention to the individual.

After some hesitation, I have decided to include one more remark that has been ascribed, truly or falsely, to President Johnson. The remark is worth reporting, not because it is off-color, but because it so clearly demonstrates Johnson's faith that implementing is what *really* counts. "When you grab 'em by the balls," the remark goes, "their hearts and minds will soon follow." Translated, that would read, "If you catch people where their #3 emotions are, then the #2 rationality and their #1 values will adapt themselves to fit." In this rather cynical ideology, emotionality dominates both logic and morality. While Johnson's application of that ideology looks especially manipulative, the ideology itself underlies the practice of many other types of implementers.

It's not too difficult to find other examples of excellent implementers. During World War II General George Patton was a flamboyant example, out there at the head of his troops, his twin pearl-handled revolvers at his side. And Ronald Reagan has shown extraordinary skill at social influence, both through his mastery of the media and in face-to-face dealings with congressmen. Remember, for example, how, early in his first term, he got those AWAC planes for the Saudis? While commentators were insisting that he couldn't possibly push the deal through, he did. And the newspapers talked about how his personal charm had swung the votes his way. Incidentally, was any #1 mission involved in that deal? Or was any of the deal part of a grand #2 plan? Most observers seemed to feel that in that case #3 was all there was.

Doesn't Lee Iacocca belong on any list of great recent managerial implementers? He may be good at #1 and #2 as well, but his affable personal implementing style and his effective exploitation of the emotional aspects of managing have been extraordinary.

Each of us could probably make a private list of "implementers I have known"—from a particular teacher who counseled and guided us, to the company tactician who always seemed to know just when to push hard and when to back off, to that extraordinary sales rep who somehow made those impossible sales, to the negotiator who always seemed to get a better deal than anyone else.

If Johnson serves as a caricature of the extreme and skillful implementer, who can similarly exemplify the far-out problem solver? The epitome of rational, analytic intelligence? The person who could decompose very complex problems and then reassemble them into a clear controllable form? Does your vice president for finance fit the mold? Or your chief industrial engineer? How about David Stockman, recently the director of the U.S. Budget Bureau?

One public figure of a couple of decades ago who fitted that image perfectly, at least by media stereotype, was Robert McNamara during his tenure as U.S. secretary of defense. The later McNamara of the World Bank appears much more mellow than did the earlier Department of Defense version. McNamara in those early years was much admired by many of his contemporaries chiefly because of his brilliantly orderly, systematic, and rational mind. In contrast to the stories about LBJ (under whom McNamara served), the stories about McNamara reflect just those #2 qualities. Here's one:

McNamara is attending a presentation at which the presenter shows slide after slide full of graphs and charts and numbers. At the 105th slide, McNamara says, "Stop! Slide number 105 contradicts slide number 6." And sure enough, he is right! Everyone in attendance is awed by his capacity to order and process such massive quantities of information. Some Washington veterans still count McNamara as the

greatest civil servant of his time. They usually cite his inci-
sive, analytic, logical qualities as the main reason.

However, at least as the stories go, the McNamara of
those DOD days was not nearly as effective in implementing
his decisions as he was in making them, and history books
are not likely to picture him as a great visionary (though that
is probably quite unjust). There are Washington old-timers
who still turn beet red with anger at the mention of his
name. When they calm down enough to say why, it is almost
always to complain that he tried to "take over," to reduce
other people's autonomy. Some generals in Vietnam and
some legislators in Washington, themselves pretty good #3
implementers, viewed him as an intruder into their autonomous territories and resisted those carefully worked-out controls imposed from the Pentagon.

While it is difficult to identify senior managers who
manifest extreme #2 posture in these late 1980s, such managers were less rare in the 60s and 70s. In those years, executives like Roy Ash at Litton Industries and Harold Geneen at
ITT were seen as the very model of modern managers—
brilliant, tough, systematic, coldly rational.

Analytic think tanks like the Rand Corporation
flourished in those decades too. And small analytic-planning
groups played a powerful role in France. The stereotype of
the cool analytic MBA also came into its own in that period
too, and it became so popular with managers that the number of such MBAs multiplied, as did the number of business
schools that produced them. The 1960s and 70s were the
decades when corporate staffs grew fat and great conglomer-
ates roamed the earth.

Examples of #1 pathfinders, however, seem to turn up
throughout human history. They include great religious figures like Jesus and Mohammed; leaders of nations like Ma-
hatma Gandhi, Vladimir Ilyich Lenin, Charles de Gaulle, Lee
Kuan Yew, and Golda Meir; and pioneers in the professions
like Florence Nightingale and Sigmund Freud.

Other less attractive personages also belong on the pathfinder list: Adolf Hitler, Muammar al-Qaddafi, Napoleon Bonaparte, and Attila the Hun. My favorite candidate for recent top-of-the-line pathfinder is Dr. Martin Luther King, Jr. His most remembered phrase is "I have a dream." That's as pathfinding a phrase as one can imagine. Of course, Dr. King must be counted as a great implementer as well. Followers flocked to act upon his dream. He too changed behavior by emotional means, though he used a style quite different from President Johnson's.

Just for practice, imagine how differently either Robert McNamara or Lyndon Johnson, given the same intent as King's, might have approached the same problem of changing race relations in America.

McNamara would have worked out a grand strategy, wouldn't he? He would have been sure that all of the staff work had been done, the information gathered and analyzed, the contingencies planned for. He would have done an admirably professional job.

President Johnson's approach? Perhaps he would have identified the key players, figured out which people really had the power. Then perhaps he would have worked on those people, one at a time, using every weapon that he could muster to line them up—from the prestige of his office, to promises of support for their pet projects, to personal persuasion.

Would either of them have shown the passionate, resolute, self-sacrificing style used by Dr. King? I think not.

In the corporate world, pathfinders are, thank heaven, not yet an entirely endangered species. They can most often (but not always) be found among founders of companies, in part because successful founders are apt to get more public attention than second- or third-generation managers.

Some recent examples: Messrs. Hewlett and Packard seem to have truly committed themselves to a clear set of organizational values. They have captured and transmitted much of their intent with the phrase "the H-P way." That phrase really means something to H-P people everywhere. It describes a style of openness, honesty, and mutual support and respect reminiscent of the best of small-town America. At Apple Computer, in contrast, Steve Jobs and Company tried to pursue a very different vision—a brash, innovative, almost arrogant organizational culture. Some observers saw that pursuit as a somewhat flaky new children's crusade; for others, it was a youthful cultural revolution, ideally appropriate to its time, its place, and its product.

But in older companies too, pathfinders arise. Pehr Gyllenhammer at Volvo has pushed long, hard, and effectively for a more humane and productive alternative to the old assembly line. He has argued saliently for keeping most of Volvo's operations in its native Sweden despite high labor costs, because he believes in fighting the productivity battle in more positive ways than by escaping to cheap labor overseas.

So Volvo has tried to stay competitive (and so far it has worked) by innovating in both the technology and the sociology of production—building quality cars and trucks with small teams, using appropriate tools, and even modifying the design of its products to fit coherently into the total system. So far, it's doing pretty well.

Ren McPherson, at Dana Corporation, has also successfully pushed his vision of people-based productivity into an otherwise unglamorous old auto parts company. He too did it by using personal passion and determination, injecting pride and enthusiasm into the organization.

In all of these cases the pathfinding leaders have backed up their own pathfinding leadership with effective #3 participative-type implementation, providing us with living examples of successful marriages between #1 and #3. In later chapters that #1–#3 relationship gets a closer look, and so do some of the obstacles that frequently beset such marriages.

Surely the reader can (and should) add to this list from personal experience. Pathfinders—dedicated, purposive people—are not to be found only among the famous and infamous, or only at the tops of large organizations. Small entrepreneurial companies are very often led by people with such dedication to particular visions and values, and deep within large organizations, often in the face of enormous bureaucratic roadblocks, the dedicated champions of new ideas and important causes still make their voices heard.

Does the managerial world need more pathfinding?

There are some persuasive arguments on both sides of the question of the importance of pathfinding, especially in large organizations. On the pro side:

- Innovations are almost always the products of pathfinding individuals and small groups, almost never the products of large, highly structured bureaucracies.

- Breakthroughs in any field typically emerge from a combination of thorough understanding of the existing rules *and* a risk-taking readiness to break out of them, to march to different drummers.

- One can also cite the usual broader arguments: the knowledge explosion, ever faster technological change, a crowded and small organizational world. For those reasons and more, organizations need both innovation and direction. They need a constant flow of innovations in products and services because competitors will kill them if they stand still. Intercontinental airplanes knock off passenger liners. Slide rules give way to calculators. Transistors not only destroy vacuum-tube makers but also displace old ways of building watches, radios, and computers. Organizations need direction and purpose lest they be lost in the buffeting storms of competition, regulation, and social change. And individuals need purpose lest *they* be lost in meaningless ennui. The pathfinding part of managing is about both innovation and purpose.

● But let's not try to justify #1 by using only #2-type arguments. There are powerful #1-type reasons for building more pathfinding into Western management. Pathfinding is our heritage, in the United States and almost all other Western countries. Our traditions and our self-esteem commit us to changing the world, to developing the new and the better. Independence, achievement, and daring are integral to our value systems. Pathfinding is what we claim to believe in. We should build it into ourselves and our organizations just because it is our heritage, and just because we believe it is good.

● Just in case the hardheaded reader wants a more practical reason to supplement all of that sentimental junk, here's one: Our traditions of individualism, of independent effort, of starting new fires may just constitute one of our few comparative advantages over the Japanese, with their traditions of conformity, obedience, and self-subordination.

Perhaps it's appropriate here to cite just a few arguments against pushing the pathfinding idea too far:

● How can you run a company full of independent, rule-breaking, intractable pathfinders? That's an invitation to anarchy.

● It's always (well, almost always) been the well-organized, disciplined army that wins the war. Precision and planfulness, not vision and stubbornness, make the difference between success and failure.

● Those imaginative dreamers are a dime a dozen. They're almost always unrealistic and impractical. They bite off more than they can chew, and they won't spit it out no matter how obvious it is that they're wrong. They can kill a company by stubbornly refusing to abandon their dogmatic beliefs.

- The job of managers is to understand the world as it exists and to deal with it, not to take on the impossible job of making it over.

And in the next chapters . . .

In the rest of this book we look at the pathfinding part of the managing process in more depth and consider the pros, the cons, and the possibilities. We look, first, at the connections between pathfinding and the other two parts of our model, problem solving and implementing. Then we go on to ask why and how pathfinding and pathfinders were put into the managerial closet over these last few decades. How did we come to the mistaken belief that the management dance was a simple two-step, composed only of problem solving and implementing?

Then some more pragmatic questions come up. Are pathfinders born, or can they also be made? Can business schools (or any other schools) teach pathfinding? Must the pathfinding part of the managing process, like the boardroom, be reserved only to top management? Or can a creative, urgent pathfinding spirit be instilled at all levels, even in large old organizations?

How does bringing pathfinding into our concept of managing change the way we look at some old managerial problems? For example, with the pathfinding idea in place, does the meaning of "participative management" have to change? How about our emphasis on teamwork and consensus? And our beliefs about the role of personal leadership? What about the currently popular concept of "organizational culture"? Isn't a clear new #1 pathfinding mission a prerequisite for changing an organization's existing culture?

Those are the kinds of issues that the rest of this book tries to wrestle with. The general direction of our argument should already be obvious. This subjective, individualistic, and moralistic concept of pathfinding won't always be easy to integrate into existing management theory. It conflicts with our deeply held love for consistency, for measurement, for hard facts, and for forecasting the future. It also often bangs up against our equally deep-seated faith in teamwork and participation and in "getting along with people." If managers take the pathfinding part of managing more seriously, managing will become even more complicated, but it might also become more worthwhile.

2

FROM PATHFINDING TO PROBLEM SOLVING TO IMPLEMENTING:
Crossing the Managerial Minefields

One of the hardest jobs in managing is moving the ball from one part of the managing process to the next. Imaginative vision is fine for the human soul; analytic sophistication is a worthy attribute in and of itself; and so too are human sensitivity and persuasive skill. But the process of managing is more than the sum of its parts. Managers have to manage

the spaces between the parts. They have to cross the dangerous no-man's-lands between vision and plan, and between
plan and productive action.

This chapter takes a first overview of the three possible
pairs of connections among the three parts of our model: the
problem solving–implementing connection, the pathfinding–problem solving connection, and the pathfinding–implementing connection.

We start with the connection most familiar to managers,
the transition from #2 problem solving to #3 implementing.
For decades, managers, consultants, and academics have
wrestled with that issue in search of effective ways to move
human organizations from plans to actions. A second and
even more troublesome transition lies between #1 visions
and #2 blueprints, between imaginative dreams and engineering realities. The third connection, between #1 pathfinding and #3 implementing, has been largely ignored in
the past, but will become, we propose, one of the significant
management challenges of the next few years.

The decision making–implementing connection: The rough road from plans to action

Moving the ball from #2 decision making to #3 implementing is a problem every day of every manager's life. The
same problem, in a more general form, confronts the organization as a whole as it tries to find a design that expedites
movement from plans and strategies to their effective implementation.

Even for each of us as individuals, it's not always easy
to move from deciding to do something to actually doing it.
Sometimes the difficulty is specific and clear. We just can't
fire that guy. Or we can't quite write that memo properly,
even after we have decided exactly what needs to be said. Or
we know how we want to tell off that SOB, but all that comes

out is a confused and ineffectual burble. Sometimes the problem is very broad and long term. We want to turn this company around. We want to change this company's culture. But even great plans frequently fail in their execution.

Individuals who are skillful as decision makers or as implementers often fail for lack of the skills needed in dealing with the space between decision making and implementing. Those transition skills can be fostered or hindered by early experiences of success or failure, and by the values often inadvertently taught by parents and educators. We aren't apt to learn to integrate the two, for instance, if we have been taught that only one of them is worth worrying about. Some professors, knowingly or not, teach their students that #2 is the significant member of the pair. The important thing is to learn to think straight, to make correct decisions. Be "right headed," not "wrong headed." Be "hard," not "soft." It's getting the right answer, making the right decision that counts. And it does. But when students who have learned that lesson arrive on the organizational scene, their naïveté about implementing through people is often terrible to behold. Recent media caricatures of MBAs usually picture them that way—all #2, no #3. They are criticized as number crunchers, ineptly stepping on everybody's toes. In fact, that isn't quite accurate, but there is enough ignorance of #3 around to warrant some concern.

When a young manager behaves like a bull in a china shop, it sometimes happens out of ignorance. "No one ever told me I would have to deal with real people." Ignorance is perhaps forgivable, and to some extent it can be remedied. The more difficult and perhaps more numerous cases occur when young #2-trained managers throw their intellectual weight around more out of arrogance than ignorance. That happens when they have not only been taught #2 skills but have also been taught that the #2 way is the right way, the true way, the only way to think. Armed by their professors with the Analytic Method, they ride (on their terminals) confidently into the organizational valley of death.

The #2–#3 transition can also fail because it tilts in the other direction, with equally painful and costly results. While committed disciples of #2 thinking may infuriate us with their naive self-assurance, true believers in participative-type #3 styles can also be quite insufferable. They always seem to be offering obscure and useless post hoc psychodynamic interpretations of trivial events, along with uninvited and immediate personal intimacies. And while impressed by #2 types, they are apt to be hostile toward them, eager to point out their psychological weaknesses. No matter what the problem, they are always likely to recommend a three-day retreat by the seashore.

Disciples of other branches of the #3 Church of Implementing can also make the transition from #2 to #3 inordinately difficult. The adept instrumental manipulator, for example, who believes that it is *who,* not what, you know will devote more energy to engaging in power games than to getting the work done. Unless paid their price, such virtuosos of office politics can delay, divert, ignore, or otherwise block the implementation of good decisions. Such people are highly skilled in what one of my colleagues calls "counterimplementation," a skill that sometimes has its positive uses. I will never forget a Washington civil servant who, in telling me about his job (and boasting about his power), described his cabinet-level boss as "Christmas help." "Cabinet secretaries come and go," he said, "but I'm the one with the connections on the Hill. I know all about how the system works. I decide what people get what jobs in this shop. And he'd better go along."

When such behavior occurs only occasionally, we can ascribe it to the special personality quirks of particular individuals, and most organizations can deal with it. But when the tilt toward #2 problem solving or toward #3 implementing becomes chronically characteristic of whole chunks of the organization, serious long-term stresses follow. If the technical side of the company deeply values #2-type rationality and logic, while the salespeople think in social and relational #3 terms, the gap between technical decisions and their implementation in the marketplace can grow dangerously wide. If the R&D people want to do fundamental research to win Nobel prizes, while the marketing people are demanding glow-in-the-dark hula hoops, the #2–#3 gap is too big. If the lawyers regularly say no to new product packages because litigation could result, while the product manager knows he can beat the pants off the competition with his new packages, the #2–#3 gap is once again too wide.

Given, then, that the #2–#3 transition often causes serious trouble for individuals and for organizations, a sensible #2-type next step is to isolate the problem, then take it apart and try to find its core.

In its seductively simplest and most isolated form, the #2–#3 problem can be stated this way: Other things equal, what is the proper relationship between #2 and #3? Should problem solving *precede* implementing? Should it *follow* implementing? Or should the two take place simultaneously?

To sharpen the issue, it is useful to set up a couple of straw men. Consider an imaginary and stereotypical #2 rational analyst's answer to our question. The #2 answer will be clean, uncluttered, and logical. The proper relationship between #2 problem solving and #3 implementing should be *serial*, with #2 preceding #3. Diagrammatically it would look like this: #2 problem solving → #3 implementing.

The good sense of that answer is incontrovertible. It's plain as can be that #2 has to come first and #3 second. Decision must precede implementation. Plan first, then act. Think about it first, then do it. To go the other way round is sheer Alice-in-Wonderland nonsense. Don't act before you think. Don't fire before you aim. Don't build it first and then design it.

But hold on. There is another answer that makes its

own kind of sense. Consider the answer that we might get from an imaginary all-out #3 participative type. That #2 argument sounds sensible, the orthodox #3 will assert, until you try to apply it to real human organizations—especially big ones. There are people in those real-world organizations. So in practice that logical #2 argument actually means that one set of people—usually staff people up in headquarters—makes the plans and decisions and then hands them down to several other levels of people on out into the field. And that's where the logical #2 answer gets into trouble. The people in the field will almost surely find all sorts of things they don't like about that scheme laid on them by headquarters. It will be called "unrealistic" or "not applicable to our special situation" or "just plain dumb."

The #3 reasoning, while simple, is not simplistic. It's based in a broadly valid psychological truth. Human beings don't love other people's babies nearly as much as they love their own. So the proper relationship between #2 and #3, an all-out #3 will argue, must be an interactive one. Mix them together, like this: #2 problem solving ⇆ #3 implementing. Get implementers involved in making the baby, and everybody will love and nurture it.

Let's not be fooled by the almost trivial simplicity of this isolated version of the #2–#3 transition problem. In the real world, it has been a pervasive and central problem, one that has deeply influenced American managerial philosophies, and even the overall design of large organizations. The logical, serial #2 assumption has typically driven toward specialization of jobs, tighter controls, more orderly methods, more frequent and detailed job descriptions, and systematic evaluations of individuals and units. The interactive #3 assumption drives toward more participation, self-management, smaller units, and larger, less specialized jobs. An extreme #2 army would be composed of well-trained, well-organized, obedient, but reluctant and resentful troops. An extreme #3 army would be peopled by an eager, enthusiastic, but undifferentiated and undisciplined mob.

Every reader with experience inside a large organization is surely familiar with this ubiquitous debate about how best to achieve effective implementation. Even (perhaps especially) leaders of nations have had their difficulties in getting their decisions implemented way down the long chains of governmental bureaucracies. During the Cuban missile crisis, for instance, President Kennedy was embarrassed to discover that the missiles he had much earlier ordered removed from U.S. bases in Turkey had not actually been removed. Somewhere along the line, somebody tabled the order. So Premier Khrushchev was able to use their presence as an unwelcome bargaining chip.

In American and most of Western management, the most widely preferred solution has unquestionably been the #2 solution. At the end of the 19th century the whole factory system was set up using #2 assumptions. Given a large, poorly educated, low-priced, and unorganized labor pool and simple but powerful technologies such as time and motion study, the separation and sequencing of planning and implementing emerged almost automatically. The engineers planned, measured, and chopped the work into small specialized pieces, just the right size for those simple immigrant workers. (It was convenient to see them as simple then.) To make sure those people did their well-defined repetitive little pieces of work, managers added on control devices (like time clocks) and piecework schemes. The people upstairs laid out the plans, methods, and procedures; each person downstairs then implemented his or her own small part.

The short-term benefits of that #2 solution were massive—huge increases in productivity, rapid industrialization, higher living standards, and lots of other desirable things. The not-so-positive costs, which took a little longer to show up, were mostly #3-type human costs—worker alienation and disaffection, made manifest through endless creative inventions designed to screw up the system. Understandably the rapid growth of self-protective unionization soon followed. Not even recognized for a long time was what may have been the greatest cost: an implicit acceptance by both manager and worker of the idea that that was the way it had to be.

In the United States even the trade unions bought into that #2 position. They accepted the separation of planners from doers, treating it as a given. Since the unions represented #3 doers, they defined their function as one of getting more for those doers. So they focused on ways of negotiating for eight cents more an hour on this job and for longer rest periods on that one. But they did not question the basic framework.

As American companies grew larger, more complex, and more technical, the #2–#3 problems began to show up at higher company levels. And the #2 view, by then the only game in town, began to extend upward from blue-collar workers into the fast-growing supervisory, technical, and managerial levels. IBM, for instance, kept time clocks in its research labs until well into the 1950s. It finally dropped them shortly after it stopped manufacturing time clocks. In the United States the deep, often unstated, #2 belief that the planners should be organizationally separated from the implementers was not broadly questioned until the late 1940s. But by then the #2 position was so well fortified, so much a part of industrial life, that #3 arguments were about as effective as a slingshot against a tank.

It took some major changes in the surrounding world before #3 positions began to make any significant impression in the United States. The technological and knowledge revolution that started in the 1950s, plus the emergence of an ever more highly educated and highly expectant work force, plus the gradual decline of the blue-collar sector, all contributed to cracking the separation of the deciders from the doers. But while shaken considerably, the long-held #2 beliefs are even now far from dead.

Over the last couple of decades, however, the #3 position has gradually, almost imperceptibly, gained favor in both the thought and the practice of Western managers. In northern Europe the #3 position received strong political and social support and moved in fast. Participation was consonant with left-of-center government and politically oriented trade unionism. In the United States the process was entirely voluntary, and much slower. As the old #2 beliefs fell away, some of our current taken-for-granted managerial beliefs replaced them. New words and phrases came into our vocabularies: "management development," "communication," "motivation," "team building," "organizational climate," and that unfortunate phrase, "human resources." The best that can be said of "human resources" is that it is a little less inhuman than its predecessor, "factors of production." Concurrently some older managerial language dried up and all but disappeared from our vocabularies: "management prerogatives," "responsibility equal to authority," "span of control." The military metaphors began to fade too. We heard less and less about such ideas as "command decisions" and "unquestioning obedience to authority."

The newer language reflected movement toward integration of the planning and implementing processes, which in turn meant a more central role for *groups* in organizations. And it is groups, whether called task forces, committees, or work teams, that are the preferred vehicles of almost all interactive #3 methods for crossing the #2–#3 minefield.

But #2 counterarguments against these interactive notions still continue—loud, clear, and often valid. Here are a few of those arguments: The #3 view means that everybody has to get in on everything; #3-type interactive decision processes therefore take forever, with little groups yakking all over the place. The quality of the decisions that finally do get made is eroded into bland mediocrity because those decisions have to satisfy all constituencies. Managers can't be real managers in that kind of ball game. The primary function of real managers is not to make peace but to make decisions, and to take the flak for their consequences.

In the United States some tortuous mixed pathways through this no-man's-land have gradually evolved. In many companies we simply divide up the organization, using #2 methods in some parts and #3 methods in others. In many cases we still hold to the older #2 approach down on the shop floor, especially in large manufacturing companies. The boss makes the decisions, and the working people carry them out. The engineers plan it; the blue-collar employees do it. But upstairs, within the ranks of management itself and among professional and knowledge workers, we have moved much more toward a #3 participative/interactive posture. There we worry about communication and personal development and teamwork. We hold seminars and management meetings. People can even take long lunch hours without being docked.

Many arguments are offered for such separation of the way we manage upstairs and the way we manage on the shop floor. All of them are weak. They range from blaming the technical complexity of modern planning methods, to union restrictions, to claims about the apathy and incompetence of blue-collar workers, to just plain managerial intransigence. In the automobile industry and other parts of the manufacturing sector, the weaknesses of that solution-by-separation have been brought home most dramatically in recent years because both the Japanese and the Swedes have successfully produced high-quality cars in factories designed around #3 methods.

The conflict between the #2 and #3 views has not been all bad. It has had some quite positive effects. It has sparked several creative and useful innovations and accommodations. Many important managerial inventions have emerged to ease the strain. Consider, for example, the concept of *decentralization.* It provides a kind of psychological pathway through the #2–#3 minefield. Alfred P. Sloan introduced the idea of decentralization at General Motors a long time ago, but it is still alive and well. The most curious thing about the idea is that just about every manager in the Western world still loves it. Even orthodox #2s and orthodox #3s believe almost fervently in decentralization. But for quite different reasons!

Decentralization is valued by #2s because it permits tighter control over the organization. Decentralization pinpoints responsibility to a few key profit centers. By controlling at those points, one can more effectively control the whole show. For #2s, decentralization thus helps bring about the conditions they love: order out of chaos, clearly defined key jobs, and measurable results.

But those aren't the reasons that #3s like decentralization. They like it because for them small is beautiful. Decentralization breaks larger units into smaller ones. And in smaller units it's easier for members to work as autonomous, cohesive groups and to plan and consult directly with one another, without having to go up and down the chain of command. Moreover, decentralization adds diversity to the system and lets each subunit do more of its own thing in its own way.

For #3s, then, decentralization gets high marks because it messes up the organization, making the #2–#3 exchange less orderly and more interactive. For #2s, that same decentralization gets high marks for exactly opposite reasons. It brings more order and control into otherwise potentially chaotic organizations.

Consider a second human invention: *management by objectives.* Like decentralization, MBO has survived over many years. One reason is that it is so broad that both sides of the #2–#3 conflict can find ways to love it. Peter Drucker invented the MBO concept in the 1950s. Recently I asked the 190 participants in Stanford's Executive Program (a program for senior managers from around the world) how many of their companies used some form of MBO. Over 75 percent gave affirmative answers. So MBO seems to have remained alive and well, even in a faddist, fashion-conscious managerial world. Moreover, it's hard to find any executive who is actively against MBO. But once again the most sensible explanation seems to be that #2 types and #3 types are touching quite different parts of the elephant.

For systematic #2s, MBO is great because of the O part of it, the emphasis on clear, measurable objectives. MBO allows for tight measurement and specified deadlines, things a good #2 loves dearly. With an MBO system, we can specify that Jane Smith's shop is expected to produce 200 units of product X and 300 of product Y by February 10 of next year. If we can do that with each of our operations, we can put together a clear map of where we are going and a clear timetable for getting there. Order, predictability, control—more certainty in an uncertain world.

For #3 types, the positive parts of MBO are quite different. The most important part is the *way* those February 10 objectives for Smith's unit have been set. MBO means *joint* setting of objectives. This means that Jane Smith and her boss sit down together and negotiate before they come out with those production targets. The boss asks for 250 units of product X, and Smith argues that in her obsolete plant she can't make more than 150 but that she can go to 350 on product Y because the new machines have finally arrived. And they settle at 200 and 300, respectively.

For #3s, then, MBO signals interaction, negotiation, participation, joint decision making—all of which involve both boss and subordinate in the planning process. For #3s, that's exactly the right way to play the #2–#3 game.

Try a more recent and more controversial invention, the *matrix organization*. It's a relative newcomer to the managerial scene. If walking the tightrope between #2 and #3 is a good predictor of survival, then one can predict that the matrix concept will survive. Both sides can find some part of it to love, despite its many problems. For #2s, the very word *matrix* stirs the blood. What could be more symbolic of order, regularity, and logic than that solid mathematical word? Matrices provide a way to put everyone into a proper box even in complex technical organizations. In the matrix organization, each person's reporting relationships and responsibilities can be specified and defined even if they are multiple. (And if things are really complicated in your company, try a three-dimensional matrix.)

But #3s embrace the matrix for quite opposite reasons. They love it because it loosens things up. It generates interaction. Matrix systems violate the old rule of one person, one boss. In a matrix, one person will often report simultaneously to two bosses—for example, a project boss and a technical boss. The two must negotiate for that person's time. The projects may last for only short periods, so new ones must be formed and re-formed. The outcome is a lovely, messy, complicated set of interactions, crosscuts, and frequent reorganizations, a scene that warms the hearts of participative #3 types.

These examples of paths through the #2–#3 dilemma don't really solve the core problem, but they allow both sides a little space and a chance to save a little face. Inventions that can offer something to both #2s and #3s have a good chance of surviving, whether they really work or not. Their acceptability to both factions is enough to explain their durability. Measuring the real effectiveness of decentralization or MBO or the matrix is very difficult. Who can say whether MBO in your company really generated greater productivity or higher quality or lower costs than some alternative (or than nothing at all)? But as in the world of politics, a solution acceptable to all sides is a satisfactory solution, whether it works or not. And that in itself is a #3-type position that would surely have pleased President Johnson's political soul.

While decentralization and MBO have already lasted a long time, most managerial inventions are short-lived. Some older readers will remember the rise and partial fall of such #3 inventions as sensitivity training and the managerial grid and the even briefer invasion of transactional analysis. Those were #3 methods that offered nothing but anxiety to the #2 side of the house. Readers can surely find equivalent examples from the #2 side of their own organizations—the new, more detailed expense account form that didn't last very long, or the new job evaluation scheme that included no redeeming #3 features. Or perhaps the rise and fall of the operations research department will serve as a case in point.

But while the struggle between #2 and #3 has produced some tolerable accommodations, we have not solved the central problem. We have yet to arrange for a really fulfilling marriage between #2 and #3, one that is appropriate to the modern organization. In the 1970s some of us found hope in the participative experiments being tried in Scandinavia (and in a few American companies), but we didn't do much with what we found. In the 1980s we turned westward toward Japan for possible answers. The Japanese phenomenon generated great excitement (almost to the point of hysteria) in some American circles. But as we have come to understand the Japanese alternative more fully, our attitudes have changed. Although we remain impressed with the efficiency of the Japanese, we have become somewhat less enamored of their management methods. Few of us believe that we can play their management game as well as they can, even if we should want to try.

Until recently the #2–#3 debate was structured more or less as we have structured it here, as though the issue had only two sides, the #2 side and the #3 side. Bringing a third side into the debate, the #1 pathfinding side, will complicate things even more, but it may also shed some new light. If we add in a few #1 ideas about personal leadership, organizational vision, and organizational values, we may be able to liven up the flavor of that dull old soup. Later chapters describe how a few chefs are experimenting with some new recipes, in which the two-way #2–#3 issue is treated as a #1–#2–#3 issue. So far, the taste is pretty good.

The pathfinding–problem solving connection: In search of rational imagination and imaginative rationality

Cool, systematic, rational #2 management styles have trouble at both ends. They have a hard time living in the same house with the emotionality, sentimentality, and intimacy exuded by participative #3s. But #2 types find it even harder to live with the associative, intuitive, undisciplined thinking of those visionary #1s.

Phrases that sound paradoxical, like "imaginative rationality" or "logical intuition" or "divergent convergence," characterize some of what we are up against when we try to integrate #1 pathfinding with #2 problem solving. Many managers have disappeared in the treacherous terrain that lies between those two parts of the managing process. In young companies, the trouble often shows up when the #1 pathfinding founder tries to pass the ball to the #2 cost-conscious new COO. In advertising agencies, it's often the creative people versus the account executives. More and more, in this computer age, it has been #1 software artists versus project managers. In any large organization, it may be the line managers versus the controller's group.

The problem can take hundreds of forms, but its underlying theme is fixed. Here are a few examples that I've seen recently:

● A fast-growing little technical company goes through five controllers in three years because the founder doesn't want his controller to shackle the freedom of his people.

- The cofounder of a successful high-tech company quits because he feels imprisoned by all the new rules and regulations.
- A large but still young company hires and fires five presidents in as many years because the chairman (and founder) and the presidents can't get on the same managerial wavelength. The chairman doesn't like the president's rigid, short-term approach. The president can't put up with the constant interference, the end runs, and the crazy ideas that the chairman keeps unleashing.

Venture capitalists, sitting around their campfires, can tell many such tales, often sad ones, about their efforts to move infant companies beyond their #1 start-up excitement toward more stable #2 discipline. One can also easily collect more cases from technical groups or research labs or marketing departments almost anywhere. From one side's perspective, the villains are those cost-happy, shortsighted administrative-financial types; and from the other side, it's those wild-eyed, unrealistic, arrogant designers or inventors or, of course, founders.

The #1–#2 connection is extremely relevant not only to the whole organization's style and culture but to each individual manager's style as well. Managers don't just make decisions by rationally analyzing factual information. Often they must combine facts with beliefs, analyses with judgment, realities with ideals. Managers have to find some route that will permit them to move between the #1 and #2 parts of the managing process without being unduly seduced by their own visions or overawed by other people's analyses.

I can't describe any widely used, general approaches to the #1–#2 question, because I haven't been able to find any. The problem, when it arises, is still usually dealt with case by case, personality by personality. In many companies the problem isn't acknowledged at all, perhaps because there isn't much #1 activity going on. It is, however, recognized as an important problem in industries that count heavily on design and other creative output, like advertising, computer software, and entertainment, and in fashion-based industries, like toys and clothing. In those industries, accommodations of one kind or another are usually worked out. Often the creative #1 types are sent off to isolated caves where they can be both confined and protected from predatory #2s. Sometimes #2 types try to eliminate the need for such #1 types altogether by trying to specify precisely what is needed. Our market researchers will tell us exactly what the customer wants, so we won't need those creative nuts any more. Then comes the debate about whether our function is to satisfy consumer needs or to create them. Occasionally a #1-type founder will have the good sense to recruit a #2-type COO with enough #1 savvy so that the two can work effectively together.

Only now, however, as we begin to appreciate the important role of pathfinding vision, is the #1–#2 relationship beginning to get the thoughtful attention it deserves. We shall return to it in much more detail in later chapters.

The pathfinding-implementing connection: Individualism in a groupy world

At first glance, individualistic, entrepreneurial #1 pathfinding appears to be almost the exact opposite of the group-oriented, participative, consensus-seeking character of contemporary #3 views. But there are all sorts of ways in which #1 and #3 might be brought into harmony. Indeed, the task of bringing those two together without fundamentally compromising either is one of the most interesting challenges now facing the modern manager.

On the one hand, a widely felt need for innovative change is contributing to a resurgence of interest in individualism and a more intense search for unusual individuals: pathfinders, leaders, entrepreneurial technologists, dedicated champions of innovative ideas. We are now witnessing a number of experimental new organizational designs intended to encourage more innovation at all levels, even within the rigidities of large organizations. On the other hand, managerial faith in teamwork and collaboration is also on the rise almost everywhere in the industrial world. Participative, team-based approaches to the implementation of organizational change are very much alive and growing. From Japanese quality circles to Scandinavian sociotechnical designs to a rebirth of American interest in shop floor productivity and quality, managers are moving more and more toward participative mechanisms to help get complicated work done.

The challenging and potentially rich question is how to integrate the #1 and #3 perspectives—how to encourage both individuals and groups within the organization to march to their own drummers while still working as collaborative members of the organizational team. The integration of these perspectives would require leaders to lead in strong and assertive ways and still build an atmosphere of participation and mutual cooperation.

The two perspectives will not mesh easily. One reason is that over the last 20 years, the #3 participative approaches have tried to kill off the concept of personal leadership. The idea of strong, charismatic individual leaders was anathema to many #3s. To them, such leadership smacked of old-fashioned authoritarianism and paternalism. They replaced the concept of personal leadership with the much blander, more self-effacing notion of the leader-as-consensus-seeker. "Leadership" thus became less and less a matter of personal style and more and more a set of functions that could be performed by any of several persons in any group. The word *charisma* became something of an epithet among such #3s.

Later, contingent models of leadership were added on, calling for reactive behavior, contingent upon the situation at hand. Good leaders, in that view, diagnose situations first and then, depending on the diagnosis, choose an appropriate behavior. If that sounds more like a typical #2 approach (decide first, then act) than like a #3 approach, it is!

So for some ideological reasons (a deep commitment to industrial democracy and power sharing) and some theoretical reasons, and also as a means of gaining respectability in the academic community, the emerging #3 participative and contingent views both rejected individualistic, personal leadership. It was, and still is, very hard to reconcile the idea of proactive, single-minded, dedicated leaders with the reactive flexibility demanded by the contingent models.

Japanese management seems to have opted for the groupy #3 alternative, one that unequivocally subordinates the individual to the group. If creative innovation is to emerge from that style, it will have to work its way out via the high levels of trust that seem to prevail in Japanese companies. It will not come from the deviant and independent individualism that most Westerners believe to be the wellspring of innovation.

While American management has been moving slowly in a more group-based participative direction, our individualistic heritage is once again breaking through. On the American scene, both #1 and #3 approaches are coming on strong. The tension between them is already producing interesting new integrative inventions. Such words as *power* and *charisma* have reentered our vocabularies, even among true believers in #3. Now the challenging issue is to design organizations that will sensibly combine the two perspectives, encouraging both the dedicated champion and the dedicated team worker, even trying to encourage both to reside within the same body.

Such integration will be difficult but not impossible. Many pathfinding founders of companies also show considerable dedication to building #3-type participative organizations. Sometimes those companies turn out to be far less participative than the founder wishes, but the general direction is the right one. And is there anything that generates teamwork faster than working together in a small embattled enclave on an innovative, challenging new project? It is not that #1 and #3 can't find happiness together; it is that this can be done only if managers and academicians first unfreeze some of their beloved but one-sided beliefs, if they let their imaginations go to work. Some ways of brokering the #1–#3 marriage in large organizations will be covered later.

Pathfinding, problem solving, and implementing: Looking at the whole package

When we add a #1 pathfinding ingredient to the old #2 plus #3 recipe, the product changes considerably. Pathfinding asks about belief, vision, creeds, values. Problem solving and implementing are where things really happen, where managing gets acted out day by day. If a dollop of pathfinding is added to the mix, managers will have to pause and step back a bit, to look explicitly at some different kinds of problems, particularly problems relating to themselves. With pathfinding added in, managing becomes a very personal process, not just a role. Issues of conscience and steadfastness, as well as urgency and direction, now become integral parts of the process of managing. Thereby pathfinding, quite properly, complicates matters, forcing painful confrontations between flag-waving rhetoric and hard action. It asks managers to put their money where their mouths are. The tension between pathfinding and the other parts of the managing process thus raises questions of commitment to purpose, even in the face of seductive new opportunities; commitment to long-term values, even when the short-term costs are high; and determination, even against long odds.

Examples of that tension between #1 and #2 are all around us:

- Our company's scout in the Middle East reports a great opportunity for new contracts—if we are willing to develop new services just 20 or 30 degrees off from the services that we have already decided to stick with. Do we grab that target of opportunity, or do we hold to our defined mission?

- Under pressure, do we go for the short-term gain by shipping that off-standard product even at the expense of our professed dedication to quality?

- Do we lay people off to cut costs even though we have, in effect, signed lifelong contracts with them?

- The plaque up on the wall has all those nice words about our company's commitment to integrity and good citizenship, but we can get that fat contract if we make just a few quiet payoffs to a few city officials.

- When do we bend our determination to see that innovative new product through? Do we go on developing that new instant movie camera even as cheap video cameras are coming onto the market? At what point along the #2 distribution of probabilities of success do we dump our #1 ideas?

The pathfinding part of the managing process highlights many such familiar but uncomfortable managerial dilemmas. Some are dilemmas of conscience, personal ethics, social responsibility, and personal integrity. Others are dilemmas of individual and organizational character (psychologists might call it "ego strength"), like the capacity to delay gratification or to stick with what one knows best. Still others are dilemmas of managerial judgment, such as when to deviate from that steadfast course or when to invest those scarce resources in the long shot instead of the safe bet.

I have characterized the examples cited as dilemmas, but they are much more than that. They are instances of the points at which managers show whether or not they're made of the right stuff, points at which the individual human being can make a real difference in the lifestyle and character of the massive organization.

The next chapter digs more deeply into the pathfinding concept, considering why and how modern managers ought to think long and hard about it.

Note

[1] This example and many of the ideas in this chapter have been drawn from a joint paper written by the author with Dr. Gene Webb. H. J. Leavitt and E. J. Webb, "Implementing: Alternatives, Costs, and Benefits," *Asia Pacific Journal of Management* 1, no. 1 (September 1983).

CHAPTER
3

PATHFINDERS AND PATHFINDING:
Vision, Values, and Determination

The purpose of this chapter is to pin down the concept of pathfinding, to get a clearer fix on what belongs in the package and what doesn't. For we are putting a large collection of ill-defined ideas under this pathfinding umbrella—ideas about leadership, vision, values, and creativity, to name just a few.

Most parts of pathfinding are hard to observe directly and often take place semiconsciously. Human beings do their pathfinding at strange times and in strange places—on their vacations, or as they fall asleep, or in unobservable parallel accompaniment to other observable activities. We can dig in the garden even while we are pondering what we ought to do with our lives. Yet to communicate in writing about pathfinding requires us to turn to #2 methods—to decompose the pathfinding idea into subparts and examine those parts. Then maybe the reader can figure out just what it is that we think we're talking about.

So we have a Catch-22 quality here. Analytic treatment of nonanalytic processes may cause the baby to become invisible. When one applies #2-type instruments, the readings are always zero. A tough-minded #2 problem solver might then remain comfortably sure that nothing was there in the first place, while a more tender-minded observer might argue that that's like saying it never got hot or cold until the thermometer was invented.

One problem: Three ways of looking at it

Given those caveats, one good way to start into such an analytic minefield is to consider how #1 thinking differs from #2 or #3 thinking *when all three focus on the same question.*

Here is a case to help highlight the differences in the ways that "pure" pathfinders, "pure" problem solvers, and "pure" implementers might think about the same problem:

A couple of years ago, an old friend, the human resources vice president of a nearby company, called me and suggested that we get together for lunch. He wanted to talk over what he called "an interesting and tough problem." I knew his company well, a service company with units all over the United States that was then doing about $600 million a year. Its work force numbered about 5,000 people. At lunch, my friend said, "My chairman has asked *me to consider this interesting question: If we could become any kind of organization we wanted to become five years from now, what kind of organization should we try to become?" He added that the chairman had wisely asked him to ignore practical issues, like how much any scheme might cost.*

The chairman's question is a good example of a #1 pathfinding question—difficult, hard to grab hold of, but certainly proper. As is often the case with questions as wide open as this one, hearing it caused me just a twinge of anxiety. Given such a what-do-you-want-to-be-when-you-grow-up question, how does one go after it? Where does one start thinking about it?

My friend was VP for human resources and a fine person—competent, dedicated to the welfare and development of his organization and its people, and a believer in open communication, participation, and mutual trust.

After a while, he said, "I've been thinking that question over for a few days, and I think I know the first step that ought to be taken."

What does the reader guess that such a humanistic #3 type would be likely to do as a first step? My friend's answer: "I want to run an opinion survey of all our employees and ask them what they would most like to see as our future organization." It figures, doesn't it?

That isn't an entirely foolish starting place, but it isn't a very powerful one either. Asking 5,000 other people to answer a question I don't know how to answer myself may generate some new ideas, and it will certainly bring everyone into the discussion. But isn't it also a case of the blind leading the blind? And won't it produce mostly trivial solutions, like suggestions for changing the colors of the office walls?

If the VP is going to engage all members of the firm in such a process, he had better do a lot more homework first. This is not a casual issue. People need methods for confronting such problems, and the time and the space to work on them. Most people haven't had much training in thinking about open-ended, divergent, imaginative questions. Throwing a question of this kind at 5,000 people in a quick-and-dirty attitude survey would be democratic and participative all right, but would averaging 5,000 superficial responses yield a nonsuperficial answer?

Now let's take the question to an imaginary #2 problem solver. Consider a true-blue systems analyst, complete with MBA and computer terminal. How might he or she think about that same question? My guess is that the question would be mostly reformulated into a problem in *forecasting*.

The #2 analytic problem solver might propose something like this: "Before deciding what the organization ought to look like in five years, we must first know as much as possible about what the relevant world will look like in five years. Then we can figure out which of several options will fit most appropriately into that world. So let's make the best possible forecast of the relevant future. Let's do some economic forecasting, market forecasting, and demographic forecasting, and let's forecast our competitors' most likely behaviors. After that, knowing as much as we can about the world we are heading into, we can make a reasonable choice."

That way of thinking is orderly and logical; but having set up our #2 straw man, let's now knock him down. The first (but not the most important) thing wrong with his approach is that forecasts are mostly wrong. That's a weak attack, of course, because as forecasting tools improve, the forecasts should also improve. And besides, even wrong forecasts are often useful, because they provide a kind of baseline against which modifications and corrections can continuously be made. Moreover, some things—for example, population growth rates—can be forecast quite well, at least over intermediate periods.

Again in favor of forecasting, consider what business life would be like without it. Suppose we *didn't* forecast. Suppose we didn't think like this: "Susan will graduate from high school in three years, and Joe will be entering Stanford next year. Therefore, we're going to need about x dollars over the next y years to cover the kids' expenses. Now, if inflation rates move down, and interest rates up, and tuition increases at x percent per year . . ." If we didn't do a little such planning, based on forecasts, we would be a lot worse off than we are. So forecasts are clearly prudent—so long as they are used as aids to problem solving, not as substitutes for pathfinding.

And there's the rub! The real weakness of the forecasting approach is not in its logic but in its soul. It is passive/reactive. It wants to know the future so that it can then adjust to fit itself to that future.

Such efforts to discover the future assume that the future exists, that it's out there waiting to be discovered. But the future is not history backward, and we cannot learn about it by putting our historical tools into reverse. To understand the past, we dig up the earth to discover the artifacts of the past that are buried there. But can we really "discover" the future by trying to pull away the clouds so that we can see the castles and palaces that are there? We can't, because they won't be there until we build them.

Our proactive Western tradition does not view the future as something to be discovered but as something to be created. Isn't it one of our traditional beliefs that human beings should work to build the future they want—and to feel confident too, in a wonderfully naive way, that it is within their power to do so?

Having rejected the VP's opinion surveys and the systems analyst's forecasts, what weapons are left with which to attack this ill-structured question? Can #1 come up with a better approach?

The #1 pathfinding approach begins by asking us to

look inward rather than outward, to think subjectively even as we confront objective reality. The #1 view runs something like this: To decide what kind of organization the company should try to build, its leaders need first to ask themselves some #1-type questions: "What do we really want to do with this company? What do we value? What kind of organization do we believe to be right and beautiful? What kind of organization would we love to build?" There are many soft spots in those questions, but their softness does not obviate their importance.

So from a #1 view, the chairman and a few key people might do well to go off to the seashore for a few quiet days, to think and to imagine and to envision the organization that they would want to build if they could build any organization they wanted to, to see whether they can come up with a sketch of what they *want* the future to look like.

What would the agenda for such a meeting be, hour by hour? There had better not be one. Would a meeting like that really accomplish anything, or would it just be a waste of time? Nobody can be sure. Are there some practical steps that they might take before going to the seashore? Yes, and that's where #2 and #3 might usefully be brought in. A menu of many different organizational designs, including designs used by other organizations or suggested in the literature, might help them get started. Like shopping for a new coat, looking at a lot of possibilities can help one decide what one likes. They might identify some designs they really love and some designs they really hate.

Maybe everyone, on the first day, should go off alone just to see what a few hours of thinking about the issues might generate. Or how about having each person write down the two or three things that he or she believes are most important in any decision about what this organization ought to try to become?

All pathfinding approaches share several "inside" ways of thinking. They are, for example, typically *divergent*. They don't converge on a single best answer but instead allow for an almost infinite number of possibilities from which preferred choices must be made. We are left mostly on our own when we use such methods. Objective criteria to help justify our choice aren't available. *You* have to decide which way *you* want to go. Pathfinding approaches are also proactive rather than reactive. They ask innocently optimistic questions equivalent to those asked by small children; questions like "What shall we do today?" asked as if anything in the whole world were perfectly possible. Finally, #1 thinking cannot honestly justify itself to others with #2 reasons for its preferences. "Taste" and "style" are central. While there's no disputing taste, there's no justifying it either. In a #2 world that demands rational justification for almost everything, you either have to be very strong to hold to #1 positions or you have to make up #2 reasons *after* you have made your #1 choices.

Styles of thinking: Pathfinders and problem solvers aren't usually on the same wavelength

#2 problem solvers and #1 pathfinders don't think in the same way. Competent #2 problem solvers know how to think straight. They can use their logical analytic skills to find near-optimal solutions to complex problems. Competent #1 pathfinders, on the other hand, often think loosely, intuitively, and imaginatively. They use their minds in ways that they themselves often don't understand. Words like *judgment, instinct,* and sometimes *wisdom* seem to characterize pathfinders' styles of thinking.

If we look at a few pieces of fairly recent research on thinking, we can get a better understanding of the differences between #1 and #2 styles. But even before doing that, it's worth noting that such a distinction has been observed and described again and again over the centuries. Long before modern psychologists and neurophysiologists, philosophers, theologians, and other observers of the human condition had already pointed to two quite polar thinking styles. The magic number has always been 2, never 5 or 17. At different times, the two ways of understanding have been given different names, but just about the same two ideas recur again and again. They have been variously labeled *convergent* and *divergent* thinking, or *holistic* and *particularistic* thinking, or *logical* and *intuitive* thinking, and a lot more. Most recently one senior researcher redefined them somewhat and labeled them *paradigmatic* and *narrative* modes.[1] The paradigmatic mode leads to "good theory, tight analysis, logical proof and empirical discovery." The narrative mode leads to "good stories, gripping drama and believable historical accounts."

The general notion of two ways of thinking, while often overplayed and oversimplified, makes sense. We have all encountered people who seem to sparkle with imagination, whose ideas shoot off in all directions, who make their bets much more on hunches than on logical analysis of probabilities. And we have all encountered other people who seem always to approach the world in an orderly, organized way. No matter what the issue, they think unemotionally and objectively and weigh the evidence carefully before they make their decisions.

As most readers know, over the last decade researchers in the neurophysiology of the brain have studied patients with "split brains," people in whom the neural cable connecting the two major hemispheres of the brain has been surgically severed. Those patients gave the researchers a chance to study the behavior of two separate brains inside the same skull. Since the two hemispheres could no longer communicate directly with each other, specialized characteristics of each hemisphere might now be more clearly observed.

In his early and ingenious experiments, for example, Dr. Roger Sperry of Cal Tech had his "two-brain" subjects sit with their hands inserted through two holes in a low fence so that they were unable to see their own hands. Sperry then presented an object, such as a small wooden block, to the right and left hands. Each subject was then given a pencil in each hand and asked to draw what he or she had just held in that hand. The right hand, controlled by the left hemisphere, tended to draw *parts* of the block, sometimes just a series of independent corners, while the left hand, controlled by the right hemisphere, drew, albeit badly, recognizable representations of the *whole* three-dimensional block.

Through a series of such experiments, some differences in the "specialties" of the two hemispheres emerged. What particularly attracted others to that research was the similarity of the specializations of the two hemispheres to all those earlier observations about two kinds of thinking. The left hemisphere, controlling the right side of the body, appeared to be better at verbal, numerical, and particularistic thinking, and also seemed to be rather coldly unemotional. The right hemisphere seemed rather slow on verbal and quantitative work, but better able to grasp whole pictures, to do more associating, and to express emotion.

Given such a supportive stimulus by the work of *real* scientists, some business school and other social scientists hurried off to write pieces about the relevance of the left and right hemispheres to the practice of management. Even the *Harvard Business Review* soon published articles about how to manage the shop with the right hemisphere.

One of my former students went even further. In a very #2 objective-analytic way (should I feel proud?), he placed electrodes on each of the two hemispheres of healthy CEOs and other general managers and also of healthy operations research–type staff analysts. Then, while they were solving separate logical and intuitive problems, he collected records of their brain waves. He compared the general managers' EEG wave patterns with those of the operations researchers. The general managers did indeed show more *right*-hemispheric (intuitive/divergent) activity and the management scientists more *left*-hemispheric (analytic/convergent) activity on *both* sets of problems, even though each showed somewhat more activity in the appropriate direction for each type of problem.[2]

Given such differences in thinking, what do we do with them? The results of some research conducted some years ago at Carnegie-Mellon University offer strong hints about how one might teach and unteach the imaginative #1 pathfinding style of thinking.

At that time, freshmen at Carnegie-Mellon enrolled either in the College of Fine Arts, where they could major in drama, painting and design, music, or architecture, or in the College of Engineering and Science, where they could major in any of several fields of engineering or in math or one of the hard sciences. The researcher, Bob Altemeyer, wondered whether those two sets of students would show measurably different styles of thinking over their four years of education in those two colleges.[3]

From prior work by others (and intuition), he hypothesized that engineering and science students might learn more and more logical and analytic styles of thinking and that fine arts students might learn more and more intuitive and imaginative styles. Altemeyer collected a battery of six tests that other psychologists had developed to measure analytic and logical skills and six other tests that had been developed to try to measure imagination and intuition. The first category is by far the more clearly defined in the world of psychological tests and measurements. The second is almost a wastebasket category, into which just about all nonlogical problems are frequently dumped.

The tests of analytic ability would look familiar to most of us. We have encountered versions of them again and again in our years of formal education. They include number series tests (Example: 19, 22, 20, 23, 21, 24, 22, 25, x. Solve for x) and tests using logical syllogisms (Example: All dogs are green. This animal is green. Therefore, this animal is a dog. True or false?).

The imagination tests are less familiar. They include tasks like this: "Suppose that tomorrow morning everyone woke with an extra thumb on each hand. Write down, in the next two minutes, as many consequences as you can think of that would result from that occurrence."

Both sets of six tests each were given to all incoming freshmen in both schools, the College of Fine Arts and the College of Engineering and Science, and then to carefully matched samples of sophomores, juniors, and seniors. (Altemeyer was not able to follow the freshmen through their four years).

The results were rather dramatic. Freshmen engineering and science students scored well above the national norms on the analytic tests, and performance improved from there, with sophomores scoring higher than freshmen, juniors higher still, and seniors highest of all. That was on the analytic tests. On the tests of imagination, however, the reverse occurred, with scores dropping from freshmen to sophomores to juniors to seniors. Seniors scored significantly lower on those tests than did their freshmen counterparts.

The opposite results were obtained for the fine arts students. Fine arts seniors achieved significantly *higher* scores on the tests of imagination than did fine arts freshmen and significantly *lower* scores on the analytic tests.

Four years of education in engineering thus seemed somehow to generate improved #2 analytic problem solving, but with a concomitant loss in #1-type imaginative thinking. The more advanced fine arts students, however, while thinking more and more imaginatively, seemed to have forgotten or repressed their earlier analytic proficiency.

The reader might want to guess at the reaction of engineering faculty members when they were shown these results. It was: "Show us the data! We won't believe your results until we have analyzed your methodology and data ourselves." What else should one have expected from good analytic #2 types?

Once satisfied with the quality of the data, these faculty members expressed concern. While it was certainly their intent to teach analytic thinking, they said, it was not at all their intent to drive out imagination. They would have preferred, just as most of us would, to see improvements in both domains over four years of professional education.

When members of the fine arts faculty saw the results, they reacted differently. They liked the findings and saw them as confirmation of their belief that individualism was being stifled by the advance of technology and that debilitating conformity and uniformity were indeed running rampant in modern technical education.

A question that the research did not answer very clearly was this one: What had happened to cause the decline in each group's second style? Did imagination in the engineers and analytic skill in the artists simply atrophy for lack of exercise, or was it so punished by the educational process that students learned *not* to think that way?

It seems probable that an active rather than a passive process is going on here, that the conditions under which we learn one style can cause some active unlearning of the other. Education has social as well as intellectual components. Consider, for example, how engineering or science courses are typically taught. Student Joe arrives in his Electrical Engineering 101 class, and the professor says, "Joe, go to the board and show us how you solved problem 6 at the end of chapter 8." Joe goes to the board and is carefully writing a series of equations when the professor interrupts. "Stop. That bit there is wrong." "Why?" asks Joe. "Because it contradicts what preceded it, and it's inconsistent with proposition X. Here's the right way." "Oh," says Joe, "I get it. I really learned something today. Now I understand how to solve that kind of problem."

Walk across campus now to the fine arts building, and sit in on a painting class. Chris is sketching at the easel when the professor comes up and says almost, but not quite, the same things: "Stop. That bit there is terrible." "Why?" asks Chris. "Because it's not *you*! It has no style, no uniqueness! It looks like what everybody else does."

The typical engineering course drives toward convergence. By the end of it, all good students should give about the same answer to the same question. The arts courses drive in large part toward *divergence*. By the end of them, every good student, given the same task, should come up with a somewhat different answer.

But there's more to it. Suppose (and it's quite a supposition) that engineering student Joe responded to his professor by saying, "No, I don't want to solve it your way. I want this bridge to be unique, to be me!" Or that painting student Chris asserted, "No, I want to paint this picture properly. I don't want to do my own thing. I want you to show me the right way to paint."

Both of those responses sound weird. They are inconsistent with the broad norms and values of the two fields. And there's the key. When students learn their occupations or professions, they don't just learn its facts, methods, and rules. They do a lot of social learning as well. They learn values and beliefs. Students are not only apprentices; they are also acolytes, would-be priests in the church of their profession. So they not only learn to think in the ways that that profession has found useful; they also learn to believe in the righteousness of those ways of thinking.

These social and psychological accompaniments of the educational process are manifested in many ways. When Altemeyer was doing his research in the mid-1960s, engineering students wore white shirts and short haircuts and talked computerese. They called the fine arts students "weirdos" and "screwballs." Across campus the fine arts students of both sexes let their hair grow long and wore headbands and offbeat clothing, usually purple. The men grew beards, and they sat around on the grass (and on grass) talking about their Karmas. They called the engineers "turkeys" and "nerds."

The university's catalog, of course, promised to educate the "whole person," touting the proximity of the fine arts for engineering and science students and of science and engineering for fine arts students. But the reality was quite different. While engineering boys dated fine arts girls in their freshman year, by the time the two groups were seniors, they were living in different parts of town and showing sharply different ways of thinking about everything from careers to politics to love.

Altemeyer's study does not stand alone. There is other evidence—meeting #2-type quality standards—showing that some types of educational experiences encourage and reward the kinds of thinking that we associate with pathfinding, while others encourage the kinds of thinking that we associate with problem solving skills. But in almost all cases, each type tends either to punish or ignore the other kind of thinking.

These ideas about thinking styles leave us with a managerial problem: If both #1 imaginative and #2 analytic styles of thinking are important to the managing process (and this seems to be so) and if they have trouble living together, how can we get them to coexist harmoniously within the same person or the same organization?

A blissful marriage may be hard to arrange, but a tolerable one is certainly possible within individuals and among members of organizations. We all know particular people who are capable and comfortable in both the #1 and #2 styles. Many outstanding scientists are highly disciplined analytically and also highly imaginative and creative. Can't the same be said for some outstanding artists? It seems, in fact, that the most interesting people in any profession are usually the ones who fully understand their profession's rules and materials and are competent in the use of its methods, but who also break out now and then, violating, ignoring, or abrogating those requirements in favor of more divergent thinking.

Management is no exception. Interesting managers know the rules and the tools of their businesses too, but are willing, on occasion, to ignore them in favor of more imaginative ways of thinking. Such managers will sometimes choose intuition and faith over logic and consistency. And because choices of this kind are usually risky, those managers sometimes fail.

Three pieces of pathfinding: Vision, values, and determination

While pathfinding often requires divergent, imaginative thinking, and while it also often requires the pathfinder to turn inward, to examine his or her personal beliefs and preferences, that's not all there is to it. The pathfinders of the world also show at least three important and distinguishing attributes: they are men and women of *vision*; their *value* systems are clear, and strongly held; and they are *determined* to turn their visions into realities. Pathfinders are not to be confused with those promoters who will, for a buck, promote anything with enthusiasm (and move their offices when the sheriff is at their heels); nor with wheeler-dealers, driven by acquisitiveness and the hope of the big windfall. Pathfinders hold some causes, some purposes, dear. While they are often introspective, they are also outward oriented. Like Maslow's self-actualizer,[4] the pathfinder is less concerned with prestige or glory than with causing movement toward some larger purpose—building the business, developing the new instrument, exploring the unknown territory.

Hence the attributes of *vision* (of some future that is worth building), *values* (some moral boundaries on how things should and should not be done), and *determination* (willingness to take the risks and make the sacrifices that will move that vision forward.)

Vision

Pathfinders look toward the future. They confront the future in a proactive way, seeking to build what they believe it ought to be. When a manager (or a whole organization) holds a reasonably clear image of a desirable future, that's vision. Such vision does not spring full grown from Adam's rib. It usually starts in a fumbling, groping way, reaching toward some shadowy dream that cannot easily be verbalized or defined. It seems unlikely, for example, that any of the great pathfinders started off with a clear visionary blueprint already in place. Whether it was Mao's vision for a new China, Robert Hutchins' vision for a new University of Chicago, or a start-up founder's vision for a new company, each was surely continuously shaped, reshaped, and clarified. But some kernel of vision had to be lodged inside each of those minds very early in the process.

The pathfinder's capacity to envision alternative futures can be labeled *imagination*. Pathfinding imagination, however, is not to be confused with forecasting or fortune-telling, or oracular foresight. The futures that interest pathfinders are imagined, not predicted. Pathfinders are realistic dreamers. They are too realistic to believe that the future is already out there.

In the managerial world, imagination is an attitude as well as a style of thinking—a readiness to consider more possibilities, to search more widely, to consider even alternatives that carry very low probabilities. And closely allied to imagination, and therefore to vision, is the idea of *creativity*. Very often the visions to which visionaries dedicate themselves emerge from novel and unusual ideas. However it may be expressed—whether in Galileo's applications of mathematics to physics and astronomy or in Land's instant camera—creative thinking seems always to accompany the pathfinding process.

Consider, for example, Norix's new "Whiz Kid" chip. Here's a passage from a story in the *San Francisco Chronicle* of March 28, 1985: "Norix, a tiny Cupertino company with only two employees, . . . has developed a microprocessor or computer-on-a-chip that operates 10 times as fast, contains 80 percent fewer components," etc. The most interesting part of the story describes the way the chip was invented: "Most microprocessors are designed by hardware people, . . . but Chuck knew nothing of hardware. . . . He looked at the problem from an entirely different point of view and came up with an elegant solution."

Whether the Norix chip is a pathfinding achievement is not yet known, but it is surely a creative idea that might well become one.

What, then, is known about creativity? about the individual's capacity to generate novel ideas? In fact, a good deal is known, and most of it is surprisingly coherent. Here's a selected summary that is relevant in this context:

- Creativity in the individual can be suppressed by pressures to conform. It's hard to express imaginative ideas in a room full of sharks or to question true belief in a room full of true believers.

- Demands that we act rationally inhibit our ability to act creatively. Creativity is easily hog-tied by tight constraints on *how* to think, like the requirement to prove that the idea we advance today is consistent with what we said yesterday.

- Creativity seems to be associated with not trying too hard. Creative ideas often come along when one is relaxing, falling asleep, thinking about something else.

- Innocence and naïveté (which are not the same as ignorance and stupidity) often enhance creativity: "Out of the mouths of babes . . ." The important factor here is the "fresh look," the noninvolvement that allows a different perspective. People from other fields frequently see a given problem differently from the way in which it is seen by people close to it. Job rotation offers one obvious way of obtaining such fresh looks in organizations, as does maintaining a continuous inflow of new people.

- For problem solving, more information is better. For creativity, that rule does not always apply. Often one can recover one's own innocence by dropping an issue for a while, by taking a vacation, by clearing the mind. That probably means *forgetting* a lot of detail, losing rather than gaining information.

- But, contrariwise, creativity is also enhanced (*not* inhibited) by depth and breadth of knowledge and experience. People who know a lot about a lot of things are more likely to put together new combinations of ideas than are people who don't have much knowledge to put together.

- Creativity is relative to context. It is easier to be novel where there are no rules than where there are tight ones. People in the arts or the humanities, for example, often take cheap shots at engineers or accountants, scorning them as uncreative. "See how creative my sculpture is!" cries the young artist. "It is unique in all the world. And how uncreative you are, engineer, because your product is just another functional can opener." But isn't it far more difficult to produce novel ideas that conform to the tightly constraining requirements of good engineering or good accounting than to produce novel ideas where there are no such requirements? In a world in which anything goes, creativity is easy. Chimpanzees can paint creative pictures. In a world in which bridges have to stand up and figures have to add up, creativity is harder to come by.

- We in the West tend to believe implicitly that creativity is the province of *individuals* and that creative people are particularly individualistic. They march to a different drummer. They don't fully believe what their teachers tell them. They think for themselves.

  While that view may be accurate, it is probably incomplete. Is it impossible for a group to be creative? to think of something that no one of its individual members would have thought of alone? If we believe—and we should—that many heads can carry a greater number of different bits of potentially connectable information than can be carried by one head, and if part of creativity consists of connecting previously unconnected bits of information, then why not creative groups? why not synergy among several individuals to produce the creative breakthrough? The Japanese seem to use groups very effectively to generate new ideas for product improvement.

  In the same vein, consider your own creative ideas. Do they all come only when you are alone, while walking in the woods or just before falling asleep? Or do some of them come when you get together with friends or colleagues for a bull session? Certainly many people find stimulation for their own creativity by interacting with other lively minds—if the conditions are right.

- Some professions require and encourage higher degrees of creativity than do others. The professions in which design is a central concern are certainly oriented toward creativity. Architecture is an example, as are other fine and applied arts. In those professions, creativity plays a central role. Typically those professions also demand a lot of divergent as well as convergent thinking. One is out to design something original, something that has never before existed on earth. But new designs, like new ideas in management, must also be implementable. For architects, it is said, that is often the rub. Architecture has sometimes been called "the impossible profession," in part because architects have to act both as #1 creative designers and as #2 engineers. They must be creative, but the plumbing has to work. The tension between the #1 and #2 requirements of architecture can make things challenging.

That completes our selected summary of what is known about creativity, but before we go on, let's put the subject into a broader context. Creativity is great, but there's a real world of scarce resources, materials, and people out there. And when creative ideas confront the realities of that world, some problems arise.

Still using architecture as an illustration, consider, as a case in point, the story of the opera house in Sydney, Australia. The design and construction of that opera house provide a nice example of the costs, benefits, and painful dilemmas generated when a creative #1 vision runs into trouble with the #2 and #3 realities that must also get into the act in the real world.

The winning design for that building was submitted by a Danish architectural firm. It was selected after a worldwide competition. The original estimated budget was about 8 million Australian dollars. The design was awesomely beautiful, a soaring structure of great white curves to be built on the harbor's edge—white sails against the sea.

Then came the detailed #2 planning and engineering phase of the project, and that's where the trouble began. There was no known way to construct the building. The engineers could not find materials and methods to handle the stresses created by its unusual shape. Nor could any #3 implementers build it. The pathfinders, the architects in this case, had dreamed an almost impossible dream; it was almost impossible to actualize their vision. As the managing process flowed from #1 to #2 and #3, that vision had to be sharply modified or killed altogether.

It was not killed. A modified version of the original plan was finally used, but the basic aesthetics of the design remained intact. A great white curving building is there at Sydney's harbor edge. But the structure originally envisioned had to be modified—reduced in size, among other things—so that some operas, *Aida*, for example, could not be presented in full scale. (There was no way to get those horses on stage.) And, of course, the estimated cost had to be reestimated—several times. The final price was around 110 million Australian dollars, something like a 1,200 percent cost overrun.

The finished opera house, as many readers will surely agree, is strikingly beautiful. More important, the people of Sydney really love their opera house, high cost and all. It has become to Sydney what the Eiffel Tower is to Paris.

Now come the tough questions: Was that opera house a big mistake? Would Sydney be better off without it? Or is that beautiful structure one more small step for mankind?

When we include #1 into our managerial lives, we run up against just such difficult and contradictory questions. We need groundbreaking new visions, but we need to keep costs down too. Without #1 we would be holding our operas (if we had any) in Quonset huts.

Values and pathfinding

Pathfinders are not just visionaries, and not just creative human beings. Pathfinders also hold strong, central beliefs about what's right and what's wrong, what's important and what's trivial. For pathfinders, values count.

The concept of values, like the concept of vision, is slippery. In the managerial context, values are lasting sets of rules, personal guidelines that dictate which behaviors are in bounds and which are out. The values of most of us match pretty closely to the values espoused by our parents and our societies; and we have acquired those values, for the most part, early in life. Although not necessarily conscious or explicit, values provide an internal control system, one that rings the bells and flashes the lights when our behavior is heading out of self-imposed boundaries. Like organizational control systems, personal value systems (and organizational ones too) may differ in their rigor, in their forgivingness, in their internal consistency, and in the punishments they lay upon us for violations.

In organizations, values provide a connection between the pathfinding and implementing parts of the managing process. The values communicated from the top define the appropriate and inappropriate ways to get things done. "In *our* company, we *never* offer bribes to anyone, anywhere." "*We* will *never* use that kind of advertising message." "*We* get to work on time." "*We never* let a defective part out of the shop."

So the values espoused by managers, if they are acted out, become important to the pathfinding process in many ways. They help define the manager as a person, to himself or herself and to other people. If we believe, and some of us do, that managers ought to be individual people, not just job descriptions, a clear understanding of one's own system of values helps define that individuality. If we further believe that morality is a relevant concern for managers, values are assertions of that morality. And if managerial leadership is appropriate, strongly held, and clearly communicated values are a hallmark of personal leadership.

At the organizational level, by specifying common rules and setting boundaries, values help define both the organization's uniqueness and the direction in which it wants to move. Thereby values contribute to vision, serving a forward, driving purpose. The values that mark the boundaries of our trail also point us this way, not that way. "*We* provide full service to our customers, even if that means sacrificing short-term profit." "*We* do things right the first time, even if that means shutting down the line when something isn't up to standard."

A strong, clear value system, however, can have its drawbacks in organizations. The more well defined the manager's values, the more clearly both the manager's and his organization's boundaries and direction are delimited and specified. And the better defined those boundaries, the more pressure there is to stay inside them, on the clearly marked main road. At the extreme, the signal now reads, "Do what the organization wants you to do, and *don't* try anything else." Leaders with extremely clear and strong values often unintentionally end up developing only followers, not other leaders. In such organizations, explorers—searchers who choose to leave the main road to see what's over that next hill—may be tagged as troublemakers.

Determination

For a vision of the future to be more than a dream, for a creative idea to translate into a useful innovation, hard work has to be done. We may envision new worlds, we may hold a clear set of values, but if we are to be managerial pathfinders, we had better also feel some depth of commitment to carry out those ideas, no matter what the difficulties, frustrations, or costs. Pathfinders must, to a certain extent, be true believers, dedicated to their own visions. Like the signers of the Declaration of Independence, they have to hold a few truths to be so self-evident, so beautiful, so worth working for, that they will steadfastly fight for them against long odds and potent enemies. Pathfinders need the *determination* to move beyond pathfinding and to push into the more tedious labor of turning unusual ideas into actions. In the musical version of *Don Quixote*, the pathfinding hero sings what every good pathfinder believes—that he must "try, with his last ounce of courage, to reach the unreachable star."

Many useful ideas have come from social psychology on these issues—ideas about external conditions that cause people to become more determined, to escalate their commitment. One well-known theory holds that we humans do not tolerate internal dissonance gladly. We try to be internally consistent. When new information, for example, is inconsistent with our prior beliefs, we work to reduce that dissonance and restore our consistency. We may do so either by modifying our beliefs to fit the new information or by rejecting the new information to prevent it from disturbing our preexisting beliefs.

This human balancing act is important to the development of determination because it leads into this proposition: People will become more committed to a belief if they invest in it. Making the first payment, taking the first step, casting the first stone, increases one's determination to continue further along the same course.

This dissonance theory leads to interesting, relevant, and sometimes surprising predictions. For example: A manager has an idea for a new product and starts its development. His boss is skeptical, but she likes his enthusiasm and lets him go at it. The product is finally produced, packaged, and sent out to test markets. The company spends a good bit on advertising and promotion and does all the other right things. But the new product bombs. Nobody wants it, and the customers who did buy it soon return it. It's dead in the water.

The rational manager, a true-blue #2, might then think, "OK. I took the risk, and I lost. Let me now turn to other, more productive activities." But the rationalizing manager (much more real than the rational manager), consistent with dissonance theory and with the pathfinding idea, is more likely to say: "I *know* this is a great product. The fault must lie in that lousy package the design people put it in. For another 200K we can change the color and wrap it in cellophane with a pink bow tied to it. Then it will sell." Once he begins to love his product, the process rolls onward. The manager tends to rationalize, to attribute the product's difficulties to external causes. He invests more in its development, and thereby deepens even further his determination to see it through.

If the remodeled version of his product also fails, what then? The ever more determined manager may argue that the advertising is inappropriate or that the test markets were the wrong ones. At some point down the road, his colleagues and his boss will begin to wonder and to worry. Has this guy become such a blind and stubborn believer in his beloved baby that he will never, no matter what the evidence, let go of it? Or is the pot of gold really just at the end of the next rainbow? Those obsessed champions we have heard so much about recently are not always a free good in organizations.

That way of building up determination carries its full complement of costs and benefits. The cost side is obvious: increasingly stubborn, unreasoning refusal to compromise or give up; a decline in rational judgment in favor of growing fanaticism; and an almost paranoid self-isolation from all of those people who are now identified as enemies. The manager's stubborn determination then generates retaliatory negativity from colleagues: avoidance, a discounting of his opinions and, at the extreme, a cluck-clucking gossipy pity for this poor character who has turned into such a pest. It's like the Harold Stassen syndrome, for those who remember him. Stassen, after failing in a bid for the Republican presidential nomination, came back regularly to try again and again, forming a splinter party, steadily losing both followers and respect until he just faded away, dismissed and ridiculed. Nobel laureate Shockley's strident insistence that intelligence is related to race and the reactions it has generated are suggestive of the same unhappy cycle.

Can there be any benefits from such a nonrational process? Yes, indeed. Suppose our manager is right. Suppose it really is a great product, that *in truth* all it needs is just a little more work, a more reliable valve here, a more attractive design there. Suppose that our manager stubbornly stays with it despite the punishment he gets, and suppose he finally wins! Those crazy Wright brothers really do get that thing to fly! The earth really does circle the sun! Now the clichés become positive and adulating. Our boy is the company hero. He has guts. He persevered in the face of adversity. A real American! His influence waxes. He is a personage of purpose and principle. Don Quixote fought the impossible fight and won!

When we cite great heroic pathfinders like King, or Watson, or de Gaulle—is it possible that we're just noticing the rare long shots? the ones who turned out to be right? And is it possible that they were dissonance reducers too? Were there equivalents of the Wright brothers who didn't rationalize enough? What happened to all of those other determined, even obsessed, advocates who didn't make it? those other dedicated designers of weird flying machines that didn't fly? Were they laughed into oblivion? fired for their failures? Or did they give up too soon because they could sense the pressure that was coming?

Although dissonance theory explains some aspects of determination, it doesn't help much with the broad and difficult questions that occupy the space between pathfinding and problem solving. Questions like these: How long do I go on fighting for something I believe in? When do I back off? When do I compromise? *What* do I compromise? And from the other side of the house: How long should we support that guy's far-out adventure? When do we cut it off and take our losses? Is the check really in the mail this time? How long should we trust the group that keeps telling us it's on the verge of a great breakthrough? Is it in so deep that its judgment has been shot to hell? Those questions we must answer for ourselves. The general argument of this book, of course, urges the reader to move a little more toward the pathfinding end of the scale, to give a little more encouragement to the pathfinder in ourselves and in our organizations, to wait a little longer before we turn that experiment off.

Characteristics of pathfinders and pathfinding: A reprise

The purpose of this chapter has been to elaborate somewhat on the characteristics of pathfinders and of the pathfinding part of the managing process. Some of those special characteristics can be captured by dissecting the pathfinding concept into the three pieces that we have labeled *vision*, *values*, and *determination*.

The vision part of pathfinding seems to require some capacity for creative thinking. We know enough about the conditions that help creative thinking to make it quite teachable. Similarly our considerable stock of knowledge about how personal value systems form and evolve should permit us to take some steps, if we choose, to clarify our own values and to encourage the development of certain values in others. We also know a good deal about situational conditions that increase determination. So there may be openings for effecting change there too.

What we don't know much about, in a #2 research sense, is the individual inner man and woman. We don't know much about why and how some people tend almost from the start to think more creatively and imaginatively than others, or are so much more able than others to find connections among seemingly unrelated aspects of the world. Nor do we know as much as we should about the inner aspects of personal values—about why some managers, for instance, develop a deep inner sense of responsibility and duty, while others with apparently similar upbringing treat their jobs as simple exchanges of time for money. And while we know many ways of manipulating other people's commitment and determination, we do not know much about how (or whether) people find some of their determination from some source deep within themselves, even in the absence of dissonant pressures.

Although we don't know everything, we do know enough so that we had better worry about the ethical use of our power. Most of us wish that we knew a lot more about how to develop pathfinders. But the moral burden of even what we now know is a heavy one, especially for educators and managers. Our actions teach pathfinding and nonpathfinding all the time, whether we intend it or not. Our knowledge and skill in manipulating other peoples' visions, values, and determination are increasing rapidly. We had better have our own house of values in good order before we exercise such extraordinary power.

This chapter has taken a moderately analytic #2 stance in trying to understand pathfinding, but there is more to the pathfinding syndrome than such a dissection can account for. As always, when we break things apart, we are in danger of losing the integrity of the whole. Pathfinders aren't just people with visions, values, and determination. They're people who package those attributes into a way of working, into a general approach to the world.

To help in the development of organizational pathfinding capacities, the next chapter considers how some aspects of pathfinding might be taught and developed.

Notes

[1] Jerome Bruner, in a speech delivered at a meeting of the American Psychological Association, Toronto, August 1984, reported in the *American Psychological Association Monitor*, November 1984.

[2] Robert Doktor and David M. Bloom, "Selective Lateralization of Cognitive Style Related to Occupation as Determined by EEG Alpha Asymmetry," in *Psychophysiology* 14, no. 4 (July 1977), pp. 385–87.

[3] This is a summary of Robert Altemeyer, "Education in the Arts and Sciences: Divergent Paths," Ph.D. dissertation, Carnegie Institute of Technology, 1966.

[4] A. H. Maslow, "A Theory of Human Motivation," in *Readings in Managerial Psychology*, 2d ed., ed. H. J. Leavitt and L. Pondy (Chicago: University of Chicago Press, 1973).

CHAPTER
4

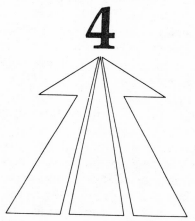

PATHFINDERS:
Can We Develop Them, or Must We Wait for God to Deliver Them?

It's easy to identify great pathfinders—after the fact! Charles Darwin, Marie Curie, Mao, Einstein, de Gaulle, Schweitzer, Isadora Duncan, and the Ayatollah Khomeini. Even in the world of management, it's not very difficult to spot pathfinders like Ford, Sloan, Watson, Land, and Iacocca.

How did these unusual men and women manage to

become like that? Do some powerful innate but elusive qualities live inside such people? Are they just naturally more creative or more determined than the rest of us? Maybe. But if we work at it, we can find ways of developing some of those qualities even in those of us who don't come by them quite so naturally.

Some students of surgery or mathematics or baseball will always turn out to be "naturals." They'll do much better at their chosen field than most others, despite equal effort. But the fact that nature is important shouldn't lead us to underestimate the role that nurture can play. Many students who haven't got such natural skill can develop enough of it, through study and practice, to become *reasonably* competent surgeons or lathe operators or ballplayers. Big-league stars? Probably not, but pretty good all-around players nevertheless. Moreover, not even the naturals are likely to become competent in any profession *without* training and experience. No one is so much a natural at surgery that you'd entrust your gallbladder to his untrained hands, nor would you send a kid who's never swung a bat into the world series.

Since few people have consciously worked hard at cultivating pathfinding or at providing supervised experience in it, and since few people who are good at pathfinding have ever received formal training in it, pathfinding looks more instinctive than it ought to. Never having tried to domesticate it, we shouldn't yet conclude that it can grow only in the wild.

A good deal is known, after all, about the teaching and learning of some human attributes that are closely associated with pathfinding. We know a lot about creativity, for example. We know something about how people develop their values too, and even about how some people come to develop firmer and clearer sets of values than do others. And we know something about how people develop strong beliefs and how determined pursuit of those beliefs can be increased or decreased. In a broader way, as the preceding chapter tried to show, both psychology and neurophysiology are generating masses of new knowledge about human thinking. Pathfinding, as well as a lot of problem solving, is in large part a manifestation of thought. Some of that new knowledge about human cognitive processes might therefore offer good leads into possible ways of teaching some aspects of pathfinding.

This chapter takes the optimistic position that pathfinding can indeed be taught, but that we'll have to work at it and we'll have to modify our regular definition of teaching to do so. Usually teaching carries a #2 kind of meaning, like getting information from my head into your head, mostly through the spoken and written word. That sort of definition assumes preexisting knowledge and views teaching as the process of communicating such knowledge. Most pathfinding requires other ways of teaching, ways that won't fit the #2 definition. Yet we often try to squeeze #1 ideas into such #2 packages. A graduate of the U.S. Naval Academy recently gave me an example. While a student, he took a course in naval leadership, which sounds like a good #1-type subject. But at the end of the course, to measure his newly learned leadership qualities, he was given a multiple-choice exam!

We can probably teach pathfinding if we treat teaching as an *enabling* and *attention-directing* process, not just as information transfer. We will have to assume, if we go that route, that everyone has some built-in imaginative and creative potential, as well as the potential to carry out determined action. And we will have to assume further, especially in teaching adults, that many beliefs, values, and preferences are mostly already in place, though often unclear and unconscious.

When teaching is considered that way, the first part of the job becomes one of providing opportunities to exercise imagination and creativity and to clarify and make conscious the material that's already there. That's the enabling idea—teaching by setting up situations that enable us to identify and clarify a lot of vague stuff that's been in there for years.

The second and related part of teaching is simply to cause people to pay more attention to relevant issues, in this case to values, beliefs, and imagination. Focusing more of our attention on those aspects of ourselves should lead to more practice of the required skills and more frequent inclusion of such ideas in our everyday thoughts and actions.

A step toward teaching vision: Teaching creativity and imaginativeness

Since a good deal is known about human creativity and imagination, let's start with them. If we can teach creativity and imagination, that should make some contribution to the cause of increased vision.

Most scholars who have studied creativity have ended up taking an enabling position about teaching it. They try to free it, to release it, as though it were already there, but imprisoned. They treat imaginative thinking as a natural ability in everyone, but one that has been kept partly locked up by the constraining rules of analytic thinking. Words like *free* and *loose* usually describe imaginative thinking, whereas words like *disciplined* and *systematic* characterize analytic thought. Discipline and system have to be practiced and understood. Freedom and looseness are what's left when the fetters of discipline are removed. Indeed, almost all popular techniques for teaching imagination and creativity build from the paradoxical underlying notion that to start thinking creatively, you must first stop thinking analytically. If we can (temporarily) anesthetize that dominating left hemisphere, then the right hemisphere will be freed to show its stuff.

But let's not overshoot! While that enabling view of creativity has a lot of pluses going for it, it has a lot of minuses too. First, the hemispheres don't really work that separately.

Second, even if they did, nobody ever explains just *how* the newly freed right hemisphere then goes about its creative and imaginative work. The closest thing to an explanation that has been provided, and the best one that we can offer here, is that imagination is just "natural." Children show a lot of it when they're young, and then seem to lose a bit of it as they get educated. So perhaps, to enable imagination, we should encourage some childlike thinking.

The idea of teaching imagination entirely through such enabling processes probably requires more faith than many of us feel. It just looks too easy. To get imagination, all we need to do is remove that constraining lid of rationality. Relax the rules; get rid of deadlines, calendars, dress codes, and all of the other constraining paraphernalia that our worlds lay upon us; and then all that creativity and imagination within us will pop out. Maybe!

Three concerns about that enabling perspective are worth noting. First, carried far enough, it leads to some far-out stuff—to gurus, grass, and religions that worship irrationality; to visions rather than vision. But if the enabling perspective is *not* carried far enough, we may be left with cramped minds that deny any role to insight, imagination, and judgment. Second, the enabling take-the-lid-off argument assumes that there really is a there there, that all of us have it, and it's just waiting for release. Maybe some of us don't have it at all, or not much of it. Third, a few all-out true believers in the enabling view argue that one need not (indeed should not) research into the nature of imagination or try to analyze it. Imagination is a fragile flower that requires only contemplation and appreciation. And even one touch of analysis will surely destroy creativity. Catch-22!

Yet that last argument may have some truth to it. While #2 analytic types have made some modest headway in trying to measure and quantify creativity, they haven't gotten very far. One reason has been that #2s almost always (as is the way with #2s) want to start with *given* well-defined problems. Given the problem, pure #2 thinking goes, how do people think about it imaginatively? So the #2s devise clever problems, and observe people's efforts to solve them, and try to derive rules for reaching good solutions. Many such problems are by now familiar to most readers. Remember, for instance, the cannibals and missionaries problem? Or the problem that asks you to make four equal triangles, each side one match long, with just six matches? Given such well-defined problems, #2 analytic methods can offer real help by providing heuristic rules of thumb for thinking more flexibly and divergently about them. Such rules as "break out of your implicit assumptions." But those devices generally don't help much when there isn't any clear problem to begin with, like when you're trying to figure out what you really want to be when you grow up.

Before we go on, it's important to reemphasize that the dominance of analytic over imaginative styles, while commonplace, is neither inevitable nor necessarily permanent in individuals or in organizations. Those fascinating researches on the two hemispheres of the brain were able to demonstrate the specializations of the hemispheres because the connecting cable between them had been surgically severed. In most of us, that cable is quite intact and it is *not* inevitable that our education must symbolically sever it.

Teaching creativity: Some possibilities

One chunk of pathfinding is about vision, and one contributor to vision is creativity. The preceding chapter summarized some of what's known about creativity. This time, what's known about teaching it is worth a short summary.

Consider, as a starter, the last time you had a creative idea—creative in the sense that you yourself felt it to be so. How did you get it? Do you know how to generate another one? or how to teach somebody else how to get good ideas? Those are questions that most of us can't answer. Creativity seems unprogrammable, unschedulable. It often steals up on us in the night, in odd places, and at unpredictable times. It bubbles up out of the unconscious, or it just pops into our heads.

Of course, those unscheduled ideas wouldn't pop into our heads if there weren't something *in* our heads in the first place, a warehouse of knowledge and experience that our minds could chew on. Whether we are awake or asleep, the continuous snap, crackle, and pop of the human brain is always going on. It's a continuous backdrop to more conscious rational thinking, though we often ignore it. Indeed, one way to increase creativity is to capture more of those ideas that are forever flashing up and dying away. As individuals and as organizations, we would do well to pay more attention to those passing thoughts, to catch more of them before, like dreams, they fade irrecoverably away. Creativity can be enhanced, that is, simply by attending more to our ongoing associations and intuitions, by treating them as important and relevant parts of our mental lives.

But when, as teachers or mentors, should we reward such associative, creative thinking, and when should we insist on logic and discipline? Put yourself, for example, into the lamplit study of an economics professor at Harvard late one night many years ago. For hour after hour he has been grading his students' final examinations. He has just picked up a blue book written by undergraduate Robert Benchley (later to become a great American humorist). He is reading Benchley's answer to this exam question: "Write a 500-word essay on the current economic status of the fisheries of Alaska."

Benchley's answer, the story goes, began this way: "I don't know much about the economics of the fisheries of Alaska, but I can give you the fishes' point of view." And he did, with a lucid and entertaining piece on how it all might look to an Alaskan fish.

How would you grade that answer? Any true #2 type

would surely give it a failing mark. The student simply did not answer the question. But would a failing grade have *en*couraged or *dis*couraged Benchley's imaginativeness and creativity? Suppose, instead, that the professor plays it loose. "What the hell," he says to himself, "I'll give him a good grade because he wrote such an imaginative answer." What then? Wouldn't giving Benchley an A simply encourage every other student in the class to think up smart-aleck but irrelevant answers to future questions? Perhaps, as professors or managers, we have to get our own priorities straight and decide what we are really trying to teach.

On the assumption that greater creativity is high on the list of what some of us want to teach and to learn, here is a set of ideas about actions that might enable more creativity to occur.

1. Reward, support, and encourage creative behavior wherever it occurs. Nothing magical here. Such reinforcement is quite consistent with psychological learning theory from Pavlov to Thorndike to Watson to Skinner. What is rewarded tends to be repeated—in rats, in children, and in executives.

2. Creativity is its own reward. While encouragement from extrinsic rewards certainly helps, intrinsic rewards can be even more powerful. If creative acts are in and of themselves pleasing to their creators, if they carry with them an intrinsic sense of pleasure and satisfaction, they are likely to recur even without external reinforcement. For most human beings, it is clear that a good idea (as perceived by its creator), a clever new gadget, an original verse, or a new approach to an old problem are all capable of bringing such intrinsic satisfaction along with them.

Why, then, if creativity generates its own rewards, aren't most of us out there being creative all over the place? One reason is that growing up usually entails giving up most of our exploratory, freewheeling thinking in favor of the firm, disciplined logic that the world expects from adults.

We won't give ourselves many intrinsic rewards for creative ideas if we put all of our time into thinking analytically. While we may give ourselves intrinsic rewards for creativity, the world gives us extrinsic rewards for analysis.

Which brings us to a second reason, one that managers ought to think about very carefully. Extrinsic rewards can drive out intrinsic motivation. If I'm doing it because I enjoy it and you come along and offer to pay me for doing it, the sum total of my rewards isn't always my intrinsic rewards plus your extrinsic rewards. Often the addition of the extrinsic rewards lessens the value of the intrinsic rewards. Getting paid for it (no matter what "it" is) takes the fun out of it, by turning it into a job, a requirement, a routine. (That does *not* mean that *not* getting paid for it makes it fun!) I may intrinsically love to do crossword puzzles. I may not love doing them as much if you pay me to do them eight hours a day.

Moreover, as managers know full well, some extrinsic rewards, like special bonuses for creative achievements, often backfire for *social* reasons. "We all did it together, but she got the bonus." "They paid off the wrong guy." "I'll do what I'm paid for and by the method that will get me the reward. But if I tried, I'm sure I could invent a better way to do it." Extrinsic rewards may not only hurt creativity; they may also hurt morality. Such rewards make it easier to rationalize one's own behavior by depersonalizing it, by viewing it as someone else's responsibility. What we might never do ourselves, we are willing to do as obedient little cogs in big impersonal wheels.

3. Closely allied to these first two notions is the notion of *planned playfulness* as a method for generating creativity. Those two words are not as contradictory as they sound. Planned playfulness here means periodic and conscious temporary relaxation of #2 rules, to enable the exercise of imagination without fear of criticism or requirements for consistency or hard evidence. If we temporarily drop the usual rules of thinking and behave as children do when they

play, making up our own rules as we go along, creative ideas may emerge.

Once again, in this device, we can see the underlying belief in the inhibiting effect of #2 rules. Kids create uninhibitedly just for the fun of it. Some of us are lucky enough to stay part kid all of our lives, but most of us take our adulthood seriously and lose that "ideational fluency." So let's try, but only for short and selected times, to increase our creativity by taking brief vacations from adulthood. How? Go to strange places just for the hell of it, or temporarily shed adult accoutrements like business suits and briefcases, or go fly a kite, or just take an unplanned day off and play!

4. Groups, oddly enough, can be powerful encouragers and teachers of creative thinking. They do it mostly by disinhibiting, by removing blocks. Most of us have experienced a few of those rare group atmospheres that somehow makes us feel both free and motivated to think creatively. Such seminal occasions are rare and wonderful—times when ideas come tumbling out of us and everyone around us; times of far-out associative connections among all sorts of thoughts, often so bizarre that everyone doubles up with laughter.

Such exuberant times seem to occur more often when we are young than later in life; and they seem to occur more often when the group is composed of close, noncompetitive friends, so that there are few social inhibitions. Sometimes such moments happen during family car trips when the kids start laughing infectiously (instead of fighting) in the back seat, and Mom and Dad finally find themselves dragged into the same mood, creating crazy homemade games about road signs or farm animals or anything at all. Those games never start with rules. The rules take shape only as the games progress. Such sparkling synergistic moments also happen very occasionally in research groups or project task forces, when members find themselves building faster and faster on one another's ideas until, like kids, they break into parox-ysms of giggles.

When groups can generate such atmospheres of unin-hibited openness, they perform two functions. First, they enable us to offer each other thoughts that might normally be withheld out of embarrassment or fear of ridicule; and second, they free us from ourselves. They allow us to think up ideas that our own internal censors usually inhibit. Even for people tightly wedded to #2 analytic style, such a #1 environment can free up imaginative thinking.

Notice also, however, that things don't always work as well the other way. If we're already loose and imaginative, a tight #2 environment may not be of much help in improving our analytic skills. To learn to think more analytically, we may have to hit the books and pass the exams.

And notice too that most groups, especially in organiza-tional settings, are more often inhibitors of creative thinking than enablers. While groups *can* enable free thinking, they are usually busy doing the reverse—evaluating their mem-bers or pressuring them to feel more, not less, inhibited.

5. Just practicing thinking as flexibly as possible can help one's creativity. Many books and procedures offer guid-ance. Most of them are about creative problem solving rather than creative pathfinding. But increasing one's flexibility by learning to look at given problems from many different an-gles is certainly a step in the right direction.

Clarifying values

A second chunk of pathfinding is about values, most of which get established early in life, long before one enters MBA programs or goes to work in organizations. Neither professors nor managers get a chance to work on people with empty value slates. The people they work on are used models, not new ones. Those people have long since been molded into shape, socialized by parents, neighbors, peers, teachers, and a thousand others. By the time professors and managers get to them, they are already Catholics or football fans or druggies or humanists.

That doesn't mean that our values are fixed and immovable. While socialization processes start early in life, they never end. People's attitudes and values keep on changing, especially as a result of changes in their social relationships. The major way that values are changed is through social learning. Attitudes and values don't arrive with the baby, ready-made. Like the language one learns to speak, values are learned from the social surround; and like new languages, new values can be learned throughout life, though we seldom become as fluent in the later ones as we did in the first.

The topic of values is a huge one. Here is a selective series of ideas to consider in thinking about how (and whether) to influence other people's values:

1. When trying to change the values of individuals, look first to their group memberships. Several times in this book small groups will be singled out as important instruments of change. Such groups play a critical role in shaping attitudes and values. Street groups, work groups, and other small social groups are far more powerful short-term value changers than even the larger culture that surrounds them. The platoon is a more powerful value changer than the whole Marine Corps. The work group is a more powerful value changer than the parent organization. One good way to predict a person's values is to know the values of the groups to which that person belongs. A derivative suggestion: To change someone's values, try first to get his or her relevant groups on your side. If a work group's values, for instance, are antiorganizational, the new recruit who is put to work with that group will be much more likely to adopt its anti-company values than your procompany ones. If a work group values honesty, quality, and duty, the new recruit, no

matter how different initially, is likely to move in the same direction.

2. The processes by which groups (or anyone) modify someone's attitudes and values are familiar to most of us. In general, unfreezing must precede refreezing. People's values do not simply change from A to B. They go through three stages: from A to not A, then to B. First, one must be made unhappy and uncomfortable with old values; then, from that limbolike state, one goes on to adopt new ones. How? Groups punish or simply ignore deviant values until the target person stops expressing them. They then go on to reward any, however minimal, expression of the "right" values. The dissonance-reducing rationalizing act, discussed in the last chapter, picks it up from there. Baby steps toward the new, approved values are self-supported. Brainwashing? Not far from it. Social influence is a more acceptable phrase, and it's practiced all the time by families, peer groups, churches, corporations, and the Moonies.

How can social influencers get away with it? Are we really that easily influenced? Mostly yes, but sometimes the process doesn't work. We try hard to pressure someone to modify values in our direction, and we fail. We are most likely to fail when we try to make large and fast changes rather than incremental ones or when the person we are trying to change already holds clear and strong values quite different from our own. But we fail mostly because we try to use reason as our major instrument for influence.

3. Organizations had better not try to teach values that are at odds with those of the society around them. They will find it hard to get recruits to give up their society's values, even under strong peer group pressure. The task will be especially difficult if those recruits go back into that society nights and weekends to get their old values refrozen.

4. It is important to appreciate the power of group pressures. A group can turn the screws very tight when it wants to influence one of its members, especially if the group is

solid in its beliefs and if the new member is all alone. The group usually starts in a very low key way by "reasoning." "Let us show you," it says, "that our beliefs are reasonable and sensible." But beneath this surface rationality, a veiled threat is intendedly discernible: "Be reasonable" means see it our way or watch out. If reason fails, the group's second step is usually to try a kind of emotional seduction: "Even if you don't really believe it, just go along, for the sake of the group." Here the group is much like Dad appealing to Junior to come home early tonight "for your mother's sake—you know how she worries." The third step is usually a sudden shift from seduction to attack: "Your views are stupid, unreasonable, out of date." And failing that, the group levies its ultimate punishment, rejection and isolation. The new member is now ignored, stripped of all influence. When he talks, no one listens. That's tough punishment. Most of us become "reasonable," and rationalize our "reasonableness" too, before the group gets that far.

5. Total immersion really helps in trying to change values. It's a method shared by many strange bedfellows—armies, many churches, some sensitivity training seminars (like the weekend marathons so popular in the 1960s), and some companies' management development programs.

Again the unfreeze-refreeze model applies. To change people's values, first take them away from their protective environments—from their work groups, their families, and their communities. Then shave their heads, if you can, and take their clothing and their names away from them too, so that as much as possible of the armament that protects their old values is stripped away. Then dump them, for 24 hours a day, into a new setting—a boot camp or an isolated monastery or the company's faraway training center. Only then, when they're psychologically naked, uncertain, scared, and all alone, go to work to instill the new values that your institution espouses.

If the use of such methods violates the reader's own

values, it should. We can too easily rationalize their use by arguing that the ends warrant the means; or that everybody's doing it, so I want my turn too. Their conscious use deserves careful ethical evaluation. Whether we use them or not, those methods are simply extensions of the methods by which most of us try to raise our children. And their effectiveness is evidenced in the cults that are and always have been everywhere around us.

6. The visible day-to-day actions of the organization's leaders also teach the organization's values to its people. Leaders often do not intend to influence values, but they do it all the time. People in authority are always in the spotlight in organizations. Their actions, often distorted and caricatured, are quickly telegraphed and carefully dissected in a search for hidden meanings and purposes that often aren't there. Over time those interpretations are distilled into a picture of the "real" values of this company, to be adopted or attacked depending on the larger organizational culture.

7. Consistency is not a consistent attribute of our own or other people's value systems. Humans, it has been wisely said, are rationalizing animals. We are adept at creating rationalizations that permit us to hold values that are logically inconsistent with one another. Killing is terrible, but in war it's OK, and maybe it's also OK when someone tries to mug you on the subway. Selling them guns will help them defend themselves, but we mustn't sell them wheat, because it is immoral to use food as a political weapon. Especially at transition points, as new values take shape before old ones are unfrozen, we can find ourselves looking very hypocritical. We absolutely insist on our new high quality standards, but just this once, to keep this quarter's sales figures up, let's remove our trademark and ship that off-quality product to faraway places. Besides it's really not bad; the government's standards are crazy.

Organizations need to single out a few inviolable values from all the rest and enforce them mercilessly.

8. Values are easier to change in small incremental steps than all at once. Foot-in-the-door techniques can be as effective in changing values as in selling magazines. The reason they work is related to the dissonance theory described in Chapter 3. People try to keep their actions in line with their values; they try to show consistency. That's why they will often rationalize when they can't get consistency any other way. So if I can get you to perform some small act in the direction of the values I want to encourage, your own need for internal balance will impel you to continue from there. Two important (for me) consequences will follow: First, you will try to justify that act to yourself—to reduce dissonance. That usually means nudging your present values a little more in my direction. Second, I've gotten my foot in your door. I can now use that first step to lever you into taking a second and a third. Now after the first step, it would be inconsistent of you not to take the second. If you take that next step, you will have to redirect your values a bit more, and so on. Thus hostages come to love their captors!

Altogether, then, many values in many people are moderately susceptible to alteration. Such modifications can be manipulated in rather Machiavellian ways, but not all values, and not in all people, and not without hard work. An organization that wants to instill a common set of values in its members might therefore do well to limit its initial efforts to a small set of target values. It would be prudent too to recruit as many members as possible who already hold or almost hold to those target values, and to concentrate our energies on their furtherance and maintenance throughout the organization. The organization's leaders had better also think through the moral implications of both the values they are supporting and the technics of their implementation.

Fostering determination

Pathfinders are activists. They don't just dream—they build; and they go at it with determination and tenacity.

Some people don't show much determination to see things through. They get distracted by new interests, or bored, or frightened by the obstacles they see ahead. Many other people show determination all right, but it may be the desperate determination of the cornered animal, or the embittered determination of the wronged in search of revenge, or the determined miserliness of Ebenezer Scrooge, or the bullheaded determination that often accompanies stupidity. Those aren't usually the kinds of determination that characterize pathfinders in organizations.

One fine illustration of pathfinding determination is described by historian Daniel Boorstin in *The Americans*.[1] When the first American settlers arrived on the wintry New England coast from old England, all that they found was a barren landscape of ice and rocks. Instead of retreating into a blue funk of depression, those tough and determined people looked over the situation and decided to go into the ice and rock business! By the beginning of the 1800s they were shipping ice and granite around the world. One determined entrepreneur, later called the "ice king," transported ice to the Caribbean as ballast for sailing ships, and went along himself, good salesman that he was, to personally promote the use of ice for making cold drinks and ice cream. It took 10 years before his venture turned a profit.

Determination seemed to be deeply ingrained in those newcomers. It was helped along, of course, by broad support from their upbringing, their religion, and their culture. In those days pathfinding values were central to the American value system, and their appearance was met with applause, not censure. Even the reclusive and rebellious Henry David Thoreau, for instance, supported the determined entrepreneurship of those new icemen. In *Walden* he waxed eloquent as he described how work crews came to collect the ice of his own Walden Pond. He wrote,

A hundred Irishmen, with Yankee overseers, came from Cambridge every day to get out the ice. They divided it into cakes

. . . which were rapidly hauled off on to an ice platform, and raised by grappling irons and block and tackle, worked by horses on to a stack, as surely as so many barrels of flour, and there placed evenly side by side, and row upon row, as if they formed the solid base of an obelisk designed to pierce the clouds. They told me that in a good day they could get out a thousand tons, which was the yield of about one acre. . . . They told me that they had some in the ice-houses at Fresh Pond five years old which was as good as ever. . . . the sweltering inhabitants of Charleston and New Orleans, of Madras and Bombay and Calcutta, drink at my well. . . . The pure Walden water is mingled with the sacred water of the Ganges.

Would Thoreau, or any of us, look upon that scene with such glowing enthusiasm today? Or would we call the EPA and write a letter to the local paper complaining about this destruction of the environment? Such entrepreneurial behavior, that is to say, is helped tremendously by social approval.

With or without social approval, can adult human beings who are not very determined be taught to be more determined? Courses in Advanced Determination don't show up in business school catalogs, and won't for a while yet. But once again, if we think of teaching as an enabling and attention-directing process, some headway may be quite feasible.

Since it's often easier to get a handle on a question by turning it around, it may be useful to look at this one from the wrong end first. What sorts of things are likely to cripple determination or kill it altogether?

- A series of consecutive failures will certainly erode self-confidence and resolve. There's no use trying, one is apt to say after a while, because I have already learned that I can't do it.

- Try large doses of discouragement and uncertainty at the early stages of a project. If everybody else thinks it's a dumb, hopeless, nutty idea, and if I'm not sure I really believe in it myself, determination will be hard to muster.

- Another powerful killer: "Look at old Marty down there in the salt mines. They sent him there because he pushed for the widget project and it bombed." If taking risks sharply increases the probability of severe punishment for failure, don't take risks.

- In organizations, determination often spawns enemies. Pushing doggedly for what I believe may mean invading other people's territories, or challenging competitive colleagues. If other people, especially powerful ones, choose to try to stop me, my determination may soon falter—especially if I am all alone in my endeavor.

- Another inside enemy of determination is rationality. Reason and resolve often take opposite sides in our own heads. Reason estimates the odds and behaves accordingly. Resolve either ignores bad odds or thrives on long shots. Determined people try to make it happen because they believe in it, not because the odds are on their side.

If we now turn the question back the other way, some answers begin to emerge. What might be done to teach determination and tenacity?

- Provide a high frequency of successes. Since success is often in the eye of the beholder, that may mean giving easy assignments at first, and gradually harder ones over time. They don't have to be big successes either, so long as they are frequent. That's not a new idea. Coaches do it all the time. Self-confidence is a prerequisite to healthy determination.

- Impulsiveness and impatience are seldom trustworthy allies of pathfinding determination. Let's make sure we "work through" the implications of our ideas before we move to implement them. Let's make sure we really love this great idea. How does it fit with our values? Where are all the likely holes? What are the most likely danger points along the way? Who are the most likely enemies? Counsel and advice are in order here, and some patient and thoughtful #2 analysis to foresee and forestall surprises.

- Provide support for venturesome champions. Encourage them; reassure them; and back them against the enemies they encounter. We must stick our own managerial necks out to support the behaviors we encourage in others.

- Don't punish failure because it's failure. Punish, if you choose to, mediocre effort or dalliance or unethical tactics. But attend to quality, energy, and perseverance, not just to outcomes. High-risk ventures, by definition, will carry high objective failure rates. But subjective success can accompany objective failure. Reward and honor determined champions, whether they fail or succeed.

- Evaluate and test the determination and resolve of the proposers as much as the quality of their proposals. Look into their histories, and into their eyes, to see whether their hearts and souls are behind this proposal. If cost estimates and projections of ROI are the only criteria for deciding which projects get the green light, game playing will dominate determined pathfinding.

- Determination isn't easy to teach through lectures, cases, or problem sets. But it can be taught if we enlarge our vision of the teaching process. Teachers teach much more than their subject matter and much more than styles of thinking. They teach ethics and values and purpose and determination even while they are also teaching Finance 101. Teaching is a total process. While the finance may be taught analytically, those other things are being taught at the same time by selectively reinforcing, punishing, ignoring, and encouraging students. For the learner, *everything* in the teacher-learner situation is part of the educational process. In the classroom, students learn from the passion as well as the analytic virtuosity of their professors. They listen to integrity as well as brilliance, to determination as well as content. And the manager is no different from the teacher. Within the company, the manager is always teaching.

Developing the whole pathfinding pattern

We started this chapter by agreeing that some of the purposive spirit of the pathfinder has its roots in nature, but we have argued that there is plenty of room for nurture too. And it's much easier to do something about nurture than about nature.

If we look at pathfinding as a not-too-mysterious mix of vision, values, and determination, it becomes quite possible to develop ways of building more of it in ourselves and in the people of our organizations. And we can use some #2 and #3 methods to help us do it. Let's acknowledge that we don't do it very well now, either in formal programs of management education or in on-the-job development. But that we don't do it is not to say that we can't do it.

A few final caveats:

First, if we succeed in our efforts to teach more pathfinding patterns to young managers, the new breed of dedicated, imaginative pathfinders might not look all that good to some existing managers. They might look like just another gang of stubborn, uncooperative, arrogant prima donnas. And they might be stomped on by the great dull middles of many organizations. The responsibility for change is not the educator's alone. Senior managers will have to do some homework to make sure the welcome mat is really put out for these more creative and visionary people. Meanings will have to be remanaged.

Second, many #1 kinds of pathfinding behavior don't mesh comfortably with some prevalent #2 kinds. While good #2s are taught to abandon old positions willingly when the data prove them unlikely, true-blue #1s won't give up so easily. While good #2s base their decisions on evidence, #1s may selectively use evidence to support decisions that they have already made. They may modify their methods or slow down their timetables in the face of negative evidence, but they aren't easily deterred from their missions by such trivia as facts. As the odds turn against them, they just grit their teeth and work harder. To encourage more pathfinding, organizations may have to hold back the fact-finding naysayers just a little bit longer.

Third, #1 pathfinding styles don't always mesh easily with #3 implementing styles either. Compromise, consensus, and teamwork, beloved by many #3s, may be seen only as necessary organizational evils by #1s. Strong organizational cultures are not favorites of #1s either, unless they are the people who built the cultures. Both teams and strong cultures demand considerable conformity and subordination, and #1s often prefer to leave the organization before acceding to such shackling demands.

Welcome back, then, to a familiar and recurrent organizational dilemma—one that was much discussed back in the 1890s and discussed again in the 1950s. How can the individual find freedom in the organization? To gain stability and efficiency, organizations have always required heavy doses of #2 disciplined uniformity and regularity. But for vitality and flexibility, they now also require large doses of #1 divergent entrepreneurial pathfinding. To make more room for that vitality and flexibility, organizations will have to make nontrivial changes in their old #2 organizational designs.

But what else is new? Organizational life has never been smooth and harmonious. The conflicts and tensions that pervade organizations are what make management interesting. If moving the ball from #1 to #2 to #3 and back again were not so tricky, it wouldn't be worth the manager's effort.

Before going on to a closer look at broader organizational issues, the next chapter moves in the opposite direction. It considers how individuals, should they choose to, might try to develop more pathfinding styles for themselves.

Note

[1] Daniel Boorstin, *The Americans: The National Experience* (New York; Vintage Books, 1965), p. 16. The story of the ice king is taken from chapter 2, "Inventing Resources: Ice for the Indies," p. 10 ff. Boorstin also includes the quotation from Thoreau's *Walden*.

CHAPTER
5

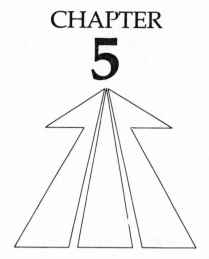

ON BECOMING A PATHFINDER:
Can We Help Ourselves?

Self-help books usually help their authors more than they help their readers. There are no recipes for making one-minute pathfinders. But some readers may want to think about what actions they themselves might take to try to stimulate and broaden their vision, or to increase the flexibility of their thinking, or even to develop a bit more resolve and determination.

This chapter, therefore, tries to address such self-teaching questions as they relate to the umbrella concept of pathfinding. The perspective on teaching is a modification of the one we used in Chapter 4. Teaching, for our purposes, is an *enabling* and *attention-directing* process; but this time, since it's self-teaching, we must add a third dimension, experimentation. To go after pathfinding for yourself, that is, you had better put yourself in some enabling situations, direct your attention to the pathfinding-related parts of those situations, and then experiment by trying out some new ways of behaving.

This chapter starts by suggesting some big investments in pathfinding that a serious executive might make for himself or herself, and then goes on, in later sections, to more modest possibilities.

Personal pathfinding: Breaking out

I know a CEO who got a guarantee from his company that he could take every sixth year off. He spent the first of those sabbaticals at a British university, listening, talking, reading, and generally stretching his brain cells.

At Stanford, a few years ago, a senior executive from France showed up one day with very little notice. He and his family sublet a campus house, and he just began to come to colloquiums and seminars and occasional classes. He talked, listened, and read for a year. If he had applied to the school in a more formal way, we probably would have rejected him because he did not fit any regular student or faculty category.

I cite these examples to make two related points: First, one way to become more of a pathfinder is to broaden one's horizons; second, to broaden one's horizons, one may have to break out. These two executives initiated their experiments themselves, and followed through on them, which probably means that they already had some of the attributes of the purposive pathfinder.

For most executives, especially in the middle levels of modern bureaucracies, taking a year off would be difficult. Then how about six months? three months? Whatever the time and whatever the method, by far the best general advice that can be offered to aspiring pathfinders is to urge them to broaden themselves. That's an old-fashioned piece of enabling advice, but it's still the heart of the matter. Reach out into unfamiliar territory. Renew yourself periodically, if not continuously. Take time off. Travel. Read outside your field. Talk to people with perspectives different from your own. Leave the trail, and do a little exploring.

A colleague, a professor at MIT, once told me that after years of studying industrial research laboratories, one of the few clear conclusions he had reached was this one: Time off paid off. When researchers took time off, whether to attend professional meetings or to visit universities or to travel, or to do just about anything else, a measurable overall payoff in research results followed.

Payoff, however, is not the central question. If you want more pathfinding you had better not want it just to help you in your career. You had better want it because you want it. You had better be interested because it's interesting, not just because it's useful. Most pathfinders are explorers. They are curious about subjects quite distant from their own immediate concerns. Their sense of purpose and determination does not mean that they wear blinders; rather, it actually encourages continuous search for broader understanding. Pathfinders are almost always rather thoughtful and conceptual, even while they are also energetic and dedicated. They seem to appreciate the practical value of a good theory. That's probably why pathfinders almost always seem to hold, quite explicitly, to a clear philosophy of life and work. They are also usually quite willing to try to convince others of the soundness of that philosophy.

Encouraging the reader to take a year off to study the history of religion isn't of much practical help. It's even less practical to urge the CEO to send each of his key managers off for a year of humanities at Stanford. But it's not so impractical, is it, to urge executives to go off once in a while to a university program, or a great books program, or a historical tour of Greece, or better still, on a project of their own design?

Even if you can't take time off from the job, all is not lost. Try reading other kinds of books and periodicals than those you usually read. Go to different kinds of movies. Talk to a wider variety of people. Go back and read some of the philosophers again, or what the New Left or the New Right or the minority press is writing about. Read some past and present poets, and try to figure out what they are trying to say. There are a thousand ways of reaching out. But self-help means *self*-help. The self has to decide to do it and to select what is to be done.

The next hard-nosed questions are these: "What then? Suppose I take that year off, and suppose I now know all about the history of India, what do I do with it? Do I write a report and recommendations for the board?" No, you don't do anything with it. Not until you decide that something is worth doing.

Just let it happen. Delay some of that #3 trigger happiness so characteristic of good implementers. If you've learned anything, it will probably show itself in changed attitudes and outlook, and only later in specific actions.

The general proposition, then, is no more than the familiar and sensible argument for a broad "liberal" education, plus an argument for periodic renewal. Pay more attention to a wider range of ideas, and if you've done that once, do it again. That process may enable you to reclarify your vision and reidentify your values.

Enhancing creativity

We turn now to some more specific and short-term tactics for trying to move in a pathfinding direction.

All sorts of techniques and exercises are available to help generate more flexible and creative thinking. Some of them are very good. Three particularly relevant books are Adams' *Conceptual Blockbusting*,[1] De Bono's *Lateral Thinking*,[2] and Hayes's *The Complete Problem Solver*.[3] All three are imaginative, solidly based, and full of ideas.

For the most part, those books and most others of that kind offer techniques to help the individual think more creatively about ways of solving already given problems. Given that the problem is to trap mice, how can we invent a better mousetrap? Let's call that aspect of creativity *creative problem solving*. Those books also talk a little about ways of discovering new problems, things one hadn't even noticed before. That is probably close to what Picasso meant when he said, "I don't search; I find." Let's call that *creative problem finding*. Those books deal only minimally, if at all, with ways of creating problems where none were either given or discoverable, because they didn't exist until you created them. Let's call that *creative problem making*. Creative problem solving and creative problem finding are sometimes hard to distinguish from each other, but creative problem making is usually quite obvious. It starts with questions like these: "Why don't we . . . ," or "Suppose we tried to . . . ," or "Wouldn't it be great if we could . . . ."

Consider, first, how one might learn to become a little more of a creative problem *solver*.

Most of the techniques aimed at doing that encourage more flexible and fluent thinking. They try to increase flexibility and fluency by getting us to look at old problems from new and unusual angles. They ask us to invest more in a wider search for alternatives, before we choose the one we want.

A typical sample problem, one that has often been used for this purpose, is the nine-dots problem. Many readers are familiar with it. *Problem:* Connect the nine dots in the diagram below with four straight lines *without* taking your pencil off the paper.

People unfamiliar with that problem usually try many alternatives, all of which fail, until they realize that they must break away from the implicit assumption that all of their lines have to stay within the framework outlined by the existing dots. Here's one of several solutions:

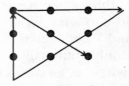

The rule being taught: Don't make assumptions you don't have to make. Break out.

Such strategic rules, called "heuristics," can be quite helpful when one is facing novel problems. Many other such heuristics have been identified, and imaginative practice problems have been developed to focus attention on them. A relevant problem solving heuristic, for example, is this one: If the problem is small, try expanding it into a big one; if it is big, convert it into a smaller form. Practicing the application of such rules of thumb should increase the flexibility of your thinking, and thereby your creative problem solving skills.

There are many other ways to improve one's creative problem solving skills. An acquaintance of mine once marketed a creative device that was intended to enhance creativity. He called it a "Think Tank." It was a transparent plastic desktop sphere with more than a thousand small plastic cards inside, each with one word printed on it. When you are mulling over a problem, or when you want to find one, reach in, pull out a word, and then associate on that word until you hit something that relates to your problem. For example, suppose you are looking for a good advertising slogan for a new product. You reach in and pull out the word *impossible*, and then you associate on that word. "They said it was impossible, but we did it." "The impossible potato peeler has arrived," and on and on.

The most powerful killer of creativity is social disapproval. Many group techniques for improving creative problem solving are aimed at removing social inhibitions. Brainstorming and its variants are good examples: In a group setting, people free-associate about some specified but broad problem, building on one another's associations. The inviolable rule of such methods is that no one can criticize any idea, no matter how absurd or far out it may be, because criticism will inhibit creative thinking.

It is certainly true that social fears block the expression of ideas in many, if not most, business meetings. The self-censorship that follows from fears of being ridiculed or jumped on are astonishingly pervasive at all levels of organizations. President Kennedy was so worried about that issue during the Cuban missile crisis that he stayed out of many meetings of his advisers for fear that his presence would block free expression and debate.

It's easy to find out for oneself just how powerful those social barriers can be. To illustrate that power, Jim Adams, the author of *Conceptual Blockbusting*, often uses a little classroom exercise that works like this. Each person in the room is asked to choose one of four animals, say a dog, a cow, a lion, or an elephant. Then, while gazing at the ceiling, everyone is asked to make that animal's sound. The dogs are to bark, the cows to moo, the lions to roar, and the elephants to trumpet, each as loudly as possible. With giggles of embarrassment, the students look heavenward and let go with all that noise. Barking like a dog or mooing like a cow is discomforting enough, but now Adams asks the students to pair off and look directly into each other's eyes, and then to bark, moo, roar, or trumpet again, fortissimo. The addition of that simple social requirement usually takes the exercise over the edge. Blushes, giggles, and laughter overwhelm the participants. Doing anything weird and offbeat is tough enough for most us; doing it in a social setting is tougher; and doing it eyeball to eyeball completely blocks most people. In developing our norms of proper social behavior, we have also tightened the screws on our freedom of expression.

Such inhibition is not just social. It extends to internal thought processes as well. We are self-censors. We often reject our own ideas when they do not immediately meet our own internal rules of rationality or acceptability. You have no good reason to support that idea, we tell ourselves. People will think you're nuts. We learn to act, even when we are alone, as though we were in a censoring social group. We carry the image of other people's disapproval inside our heads.

It is not surprising, therefore, that so many of the techniques for encouraging creative problem solving focus mostly on the temporary removal of both internal and social censors. It's that enabling idea again. Many creativity-enhancing methods start by trying to abrogate the usual rules of logic and consistency. Then, it is widely believed, we will be free to think creatively, unfettered by rational censorship. Then we can think like children at play, rather than like adults at work.

This faith that creativity will emerge when the rational sentries are off duty is part of a deeper faith that creativity is there inside us to begin with—that it's just waiting to be let out. So relax the rules, get drunk, go away for a while, anesthetize the left hemisphere. Then you will solve problems more creatively.

Some proponents of creativity-enhancing methods seem to apply those beliefs wisely and others rather foolishly. Some are enamored of an almost mystical vision of innocent childhood, unencumbered by the shackles of education and socialization. Childhood, for them, is the font of all creativity. Others—and I am on their side—insist that wider experience and greater knowledge must accompany free, divergent, associative thinking. They want the painter to master his materials, to do representational painting before taking off into impressionism. The goal is to get rid of censorship, whether external or internal, not to get rid of knowledge and experience.

Creative problem finding

The boundaries that separate creative problem *solving* from creative problem *finding* are fuzzy. Problem finding is more about recognizing and identifying problems than about solving already existing problems.

All of us know a good deal about *non*creative problem finding. In fact, most executives would laugh aloud if someone were to tell them that they ought to learn to be better problem finders. Finding problems is the last thing they're worried about. All we have to do to find problems is to look at our appointment calendar and at our telephone messages each morning—problems found! Add a few more phone calls as the day progresses, and a few colleagues stopping by, and some new assignments that emerged from those last two meetings, and we have found enough problems to take care of us for a good while. Other people find problems for managers—their colleagues, bosses, and customers. Deadlines and routines bring still other problems to them; and discrepancies between targets and performance generate other problems; and so on and on.[4] Problems find managers, it seems, rather than the other way around.

But those are reactive kinds of problem finding. Creative problem finding is proactive. It starts with the finder, not with the noisy barrage of problems imposed by the surrounding world. The creative question is this one: How does the manager actively find interesting, important, and worthwhile problems?

Adams has offered some helpful techniques that cross over from problem solving into this land of creative problem finding. He suggests, for example, making a "bug list." Write down anything you can think of that "bugs" you. Perhaps for you it's trash in the street, or telephone solicitors, or bookmarks that fall out of books, or waiters who ignore you, or useless meetings. Then treat each item on the list as a problem. Now, having found problems, you are back to problem *solving*. Free-associate (or use your list of heuristics) to try to help solve each one. For example, for trash in the streets, how about paper that dissolves in the rain or in sunlight? or electronic mail (from using the heuristic of enlarging small problems)? Or how about sticky but easily removable bookmarks? That's purportedly how someone at 3M came up with the tremendously useful and profitable Post-it notepads.

In a similar vein, consider the following experiment.[5] We send an advanced art student into a room with two tables, one clear and the other stacked with a collection of random objects: padlocks, vases, dried flowers, can openers, oranges, and on and on. The student is given an easel, paint, and brushes. We ask the student to take no more than two hours to select any objects from the junk table, arrange them as he or she wishes on the clean table, and then paint a picture. We do this with many students, videotaping them as they work. We then hand over the finished paintings to a panel of senior professional artists, asking them to judge the quality of each painting.

The videotapes show some students approaching the task in an orderly and straightforward way. They study the array of objects, select the ones they want, work out the arrangement they prefer, and then paint the picture. The panel usually gives the work of those students *low* ratings.

The students whose work receives the highest ratings tackle their work quite differently. They select objects, arrange them, start to paint, stop, rearrange the objects or abandon some and select new ones, paint out what they have painted, start again, and at the end of the two hours reluctantly turn in a painting that they consider unfinished.

The high-scoring students, that is, approach creative problem finding in a loose, cut-and-try way almost opposite to what most of us have been taught about good problem *solving*. Their thinking appears to be disorderly, unsystematic, messy. They don't plan it all the way through and then do it. They mix everything up. And they continuously reexamine things from different angles. On this divergent task, the students who think straight get low grades; the ones who think "crooked" do better.

But that thinking is not as crooked as it looks. It is not thoughtless. All of that modifying and restarting is anchored by some implicit standard inside those students' heads. They, like many managers, can't tell you what they like, but they really do recognize it when they see it. They use their internal sense of what is right or good as a yardstick against which each temporary and tentative effort is compared, and from which it is changed, until they get what they feel is right.

A similar method is often used by first-class interviewers. Instead of using the standard process of preparing a carefully planned set of questions, collecting the answers, and *then* using those answers to make a decision, some interviewers do the reverse. They let their excellent internal computers make a quick judgment, often in the first 30 seconds of the interview (as we all do when we meet a stranger for the first time). Then they treat that initial judgment as a tentative hypothesis, using follow-up questions to check it out and to modify it. That's a way of exploiting our human natures, instead of denying them. Rather than reject the "natural" tendency to make quick and dirty judgments in favor of doing what the #2 books tell us to do, those interviewers take advantage of that powerful human capacity to make such total judgments. But the wise ones treat those judgments as tentative and modifiable, not as fixed and absolute truths.

Most of what we consider managerial "common sense" or "good judgment" works that way, doesn't it? We can't specify our decision rules, but we can make a quick ballpark judgment and then fiddle with it until it feels just about right.

Other "languages" of thought can play an important role in creative thinking. Creativity is not limited to the verbal mode. We use our eyes, ears, and our empathetic sense too. While we may have to use verbal language to communicate our thoughts, we can think those thoughts in quite different languages. Creative searching and finding processes frequently occur in visual or tactual or other nonverbal forms. So let's not ignore those images that are hard to describe in words, or the sensations, physical and emotional, that are a part of our everyday life.

A few occupations, journalism for example, routinely require a good deal of creative problem finding. Good reporters don't just cover fires, crimes, and political crises. They don't just report facts. They notice things. They search for and find stories where others would not have found them. Unlike problem solvers, they look for interesting problems as well as interesting answers.

Creative problem making

In one of its many connotations, *making* means *fabricating*, which can mean *creating out of whole cloth*, which can come close to meaning *lying*. Some of those problem finding journalists, for instance, occasionally go beyond *problem finding* to *creative problem making,* and that can get them into trouble. They manufacture phony stories out of whole cloth. Remember the reporter at the *Washington Post* who won a Pulitzer prize for a tear-jerking series (entirely fabricated) about a little boy's problems? That was a case of the downside of creative problem making!

The upside is originality. In one sense, nothing can ever be original. Anything we can imagine is some composite of our experiences. The monsters in nightmares are mostly quite unoriginal. Like most real animals, they have scales and armor and eyes and mouths and legs and tails. The imagined inhabitants of other planets always seem to look like some concoction of humans, insects, and jellyfish. In another sense, however, some people do think more originally than others. Their imaginations are more fertile, often envisioning things that aren't yet but might be.

Creative problem making is the imaginative invention of interesting problems. It is not just the province of dreams or science fiction writers; it is also the province of many scientists, artists, inventors, entrepreneurs, and managers. Creative problem makers are curious. They try combinations never tried before. It is the CPMs of the world who envision xerography or heavier-than-air flight or instant coffee or governments of, by, and for the people.

In its managerial forms, creative problem making is usually connected closely with creative problem finding. The difference is in what problem makers do after they have found or noticed things. Creative problem makers put together the things they have found in new ways. They manufacture new problems by marrying ideas previously unmarried or even unfound. Could the fact that X is green and Y is white mean that Z might really turn out to be pink?

The teaching methods that help most with creative problem making are mostly pure enabling methods, methods like relaxation and meditation. These methods assert, or at least imply, that creative problem making is enabled, although not caused, by turning off the rules of reason. Turn off the rule that requires consistency between what you say today and what you said yesterday. Turn off the need to provide evidence for your opinions. Turn off the requirement that you must be sensible. Go the nonsensible route. Try being just a little bit flaky, as when you're completely relaxed, or when you're falling asleep, or when you're having a high time with good friends.

If everyone in the organization goes that flaky route most of the time (or even much of the time), I'll put my money somewhere else, thank you. But if no one in the company does any of that any of the time, I'll also put my money somewhere else. And right now, most companies suffer more from a shortage than an excess of creative problem making.

Can you learn creative problem making? Sure you can. When I was an undergraduate, one of my professors used to bug us constantly with this limerick:

> *There once was a man who said, "Why*
> *Can't I look in my ear with my eye?*
> *I'm sure I could do it*
> *If I set my mind to it.*
> *You never can tell 'til you try."*

Values

Pathfinding is not just about creativity. It is also about values. But unlike creative thinking, values are beliefs, not processes. There are no techniques for giving yourself better values. Your values are your values. You acquired their basic outlines when you were young, from parents, peers, teachers, and television. Values continue to change throughout life, usually incrementally, but occasionally the change can be radical and sudden. It's probably fairer to say that your values are changed than that you change them. While we are not entirely passive recipients of our values, they are mostly shaped by the world around us, by forces that are forever banging away at us. The active part we play is in selecting which of all those value-shaping stimuli to pay attention to. That's one place where each of us can exercise a little proactive control.

In the 1950s David Riesman, in his book *The Lonely Crowd*,[6] described three sources of values that might help us to think about which kinds of pressuring stimuli to respond to. He described the decline of *tradition-directedness* (believing in something, as in the song from *Fiddler on the Roof*, just because it's traditional in your culture to believe in it) and of *inner-directedness* (believing in it because we, within ourselves, feel it to be right) and the growth of *other-directedness* (believing in it because our contemporaries tell us it's right). More recently the psychiatrist Karl Menninger has called, in a related way, for a renewal of the almost lost idea of sin, a kind of inner-directed morality.

Aspiring pathfinders would do well to attend most to inner-directed values, some to tradition-directed values, and very, very little to other-directed values. They also need to identify the things that they believe to be just plain sinful.

Though it doesn't make much sense to talk about self-development of values, it does make sense to talk about clarifying the values you already have. For our values are apt to be more implicit than explicit, more unknown to us than known. By bringing them to the surface, we can perhaps better organize our priorities.

Unfortunately, even the clarification of our values is not always a voluntary process. Surely the most powerful clarifiers of our values are the major crises that we inevitably encounter during our lives. Infantrymen clarify their values in their foxholes. Cancer patients almost invariably report major reassessments of what is and isn't important following the diagnosis of a malignancy. Less life-threatening crises—career change, marriage or divorce, or getting fired—also start up such rethinking.

We can do something similar voluntarily by stopping long enough to imagine such inevitable crises, using that imagined state as a stimulus to introspection. Such simulated crises are not good substitutes for the real thing, but they're a lot less dangerous. One such exercise has been used in many contexts. It asks people to write their own obituaries. Imagine, the exercise requires, the time of your departure from this world, and then write the obituary that might appear in a newspaper at that time. By imagining ourselves looking back over our lives, we get a chance to think about what is or is not important.

My students have found that a helpful exercise. It forces them to think about things that they don't otherwise think about: What do I want to do with my life? What do I really mean by success? What are my core values? In class, we usually follow up by asking groups of students to read and discuss one another's obituaries, looking for differences and similarities and trying to figure out what underlies them.

Beyond those, there are a number of gimmicks that might help us to get a better picture of our value priorities. For example:

- Take an hour to think about how your beliefs differ from those of your parents. If you can spot some key differences, you might get a clearer picture of what's important to you.

- Try the same thing again, but this time try making a list of the differences between your beliefs and those of your boss or those of your immediate subordinates.

- Think about what you have read, heard, or seen lately that has made you really furious (or look over your "bug" list). Tax evasion by the rich? Overcharges on government contracts? Student protests? Low-quality product shipped by your company? The way someone you know was laid off? Then look for a pattern. Are there a few values that all of those things violate?

- Review ethical dilemmas that you have encountered, or imagine some that you might encounter. Would you donate one of your kidneys to a dying relative? Would you have stood up to the SS if you had been a German citizen in 1940? Did you shut up or talk back the last time a good customer asked you to do something you felt was wrong? Or did you convince yourself that it wasn't really wrong?

Such devices may help a little, but the general idea is what's important. To help clarify our value priorities, let's talk and think about our values in the normal course of everyday life. Let's raise those itchy ethical questions instead of avoiding them. Let's question authority when authority wants us to do things that make us feel uncomfortable. Let's notice what we are doing and ask whether that is what we feel we ought to be doing.

Determination

Chapter 3 described how outside forces can increase our determination by exploiting our poor tolerance for dissonance. We can also turn our knowledge of dissonance theory to our own advantage to help us build our determination and resolve for ourselves. The rule of thumb becomes: If you want to increase your determination to do something, stick your neck out and do a little of it. That will make you justify what you have done, thereby increasing your determination to do more of it, which will require further justification, and so on. When we use that process on ourselves, it becomes a kind of confidence game in which we are both the con artist and the victim.

One problem with building such leveraged determination is that it often becomes transparently obvious to outsiders that what looks like determination is really stubborn and defensive self-justification. There's a perceptible difference between immutable unwillingness to hear anything disturbing and determination to push one's ideas through to completion. While pathfinders often behave stubbornly, their stubbornness is seldom defensive. It is a product of self-confidence, not self-entrapment in a recurring cycle of rationalizations.

No one has done much research on such inner-driven determination beyond trying to measure individual differences in perseverance. However, inner-driven determination seems to be associated with confidence in oneself and in one's ideas, and all you have to do to build self-confidence is to be sure that you're successful most of the time!

To build confidence in your ideas, a few heuristic guidelines like these may be of help:

● Don't rush to follow through on an idea until you, by yourself, find yourself getting excited about it. If you are going to become a champion of a new idea, a new method, or a new product, make sure you're a believer *before* you become a preacher. If your boss wants you to champion it and you don't believe in it, say no. The organizational world can usually spot and discount promoters who aren't committed to what they promote, as well as promoters who have rationalized their way into belief.

● Be selective. If you feel dedicated to too many new ideas, you will be seen, correctly, as a butterfly rather than as a determined leader.

● Look back through your own history for ideas that you have championed in the past. What drove your commitment? You might discover that a particular class of ideas has recurrently excited you.

- And most important of all, don't let the world grind you down. If you believe it, hold on to it.

The observant reader will notice that these rules of thumb don't seem to mesh very well with current ideas about how to play the game of organizational politics. If you stick to your values, will you look like a naive patsy in that tough world out there? I think not. It's not the managerial chameleons who become the great leaders of organizations. More often it is people with a few deeply held beliefs accompanied by a determination to see them through. They are apt to be competent political tacticians too, but they aren't people who will sell their principles for a stock option.

Once again, can pathfinding be self-taught?

Most of us aren't about to become Winston Churchills or Albert Einsteins, no matter how hard we try. But can we learn to think more creatively? Can we scan bigger areas of the world than we have until now? Can we break out of our routines periodically to gain different perspectives? Can we learn to be more determined, less easily discouraged, in our chosen endeavors?

Why not? If we don't do it for ourselves, who will do it for us?

But how do we go about doing such things? Mostly in the same way we learn to swim: by putting ourselves into appropriate environments (like water) and then experimenting, practicing, and paying attention to what we are doing.

Besides, who in the world has ever been in a better position to try out more pathfinding behaviors than the educated, intelligent, affluent, and autonomous readers of this book?

The focus in the next chapter shifts from the individual to the organization; seeking possible roots to new equilibria between the simultaneous pressures for stability and change. How can organizations build healthy and productive relationships among the #1, #2, and #3 parts of the managing process?

Notes

[1] James Adams, *Conceptual Blockbusting: A Guide to Better Ideas* (San Francisco: Freeman, 1974).

[2] Edward De Bono, *Lateral Thinking for Management: A Handbook of Creativity* (New York: American Management Association, 1971).

[3] John R. Hayes, *The Complete Problem Solver* (Philadelphia: Franklin Institute Press, 1981).

[4] Many years ago Professor William Pounds pointed to these several sources of managers' problems in his doctoral dissertation, "The Process of Problem Finding." It was published in the *Industrial Management Review*, Fall 1969.

[5] This experiment was part of a broader study by two psychologists at the University of Chicago. It is described fully in Jacob W. Getzels and Mihaly Csikszentmihalyi, *The Creative Vision: A Longitudinal Study of Problem Finding in Art* (New York: John Wiley & Sons, 1976).

[6] David Riesman, *The Lonely Crowd* (Garden City, N.Y.: Doubleday, 1953).

CHAPTER
6

PATHFINDERS INSIDE THE ORGANIZATION:
Is There Room at the Inn?

So far, this book has identified mostly eminent and famous pathfinders—founders and kings, great men and women who have transformed the world. We have pointed to rare, wonderful, and troublesome pathfinding personalities, always innovative and determined and often stubborn and unyielding. But most of us will not be mentioned in our children's history books, nor have we founded the institutions in which we work. Instead, we spend our working lives deep inside organizations founded by others long ago, doing our work, playing by the rules, conforming to the demands of the system.

Indeed, conformity seems to be an inseparable requirement of organizational life. Back in the 1950s many observers of American management worried about excessive organizational pressures toward conformity, and about the loss of individual initiative that those pressures threatened. In those days the phrase "organization man" became an epithet. Now, in the late 1980s, the tension between individualism and organizational pressures to conform is in the forefront once again. We observe unacceptable (to Western eyes) levels of conformity in Japanese organizations (the Japanese refer to "company men," and do so approvingly), and we in the West ascribe some of the decline in our own innovativeness to the debilitating effect of the old pressures to stay in line.

This chapter examines that familiar question in its contemporary context: How can individuals find freedom to imagine and innovate inside those high, thick organizational walls? In earlier years the concerns that underlay that question were mostly moral and social—concerns about human rights and human dignity. While those underlying issues remain at least as important as ever, this chapter aims mostly at some other currently important aspects of the same basic question. This time, our concerns are with such issues as leadership (Under what conditions is it possible for individual leaders to emerge at all levels of large organizations?) and creativity (How can individual creativity be fostered inside giant bureaucracies?).

Here are some relevant and more specific questions:

1. Do large organizations need pathfinding now more than they have in the recent past? If so, why?

2. Organizations, almost by definition, demand conformity and obedience from their members. How can they make room (except at the very top) for free-spirited #1 pathfinders?

3. A closely related question: If an organization is led by a pathfinder at the top, how can that leader avoid discouraging pathfinding at other levels? Don't strong leaders require their followers to act like followers, not leaders?

4. If a company does encourage its people, at all levels, to think and act a little more entrepreneurially and imaginatively, won't that just move the company toward anarchy? Won't it tend to erode the control and discipline that are so critical to efficient performance? Wouldn't conflict, disorder, and chaos inevitably follow? Or, to put it another way, how would you like to try to manage a pack of pathfinders?

5. What about the connection between #1 and #3, between pathfinding and implementing? A strong #3 participative movement seems to be on the rise everywhere in the organizational world. Don't participative approaches require quite the opposite of the pathfinding style? Approaches of this kind emphasize cooperation and teamwork, along with considerable subordination of the individual to the interests of the group. How can such #3-type groupy, collaborative styles tolerate the persistent and insistent rugged individualism implied by pathfinding styles?

6. How about #1 pathfinding versus orderly #2 problem solving? How can an organization build and maintain systematic and orderly planning and control systems if its people are forever experimenting with ways of doing old things differently, and also trying to do altogether new things? Planning and control require discipline, regularity, and predictability over fairly long periods of time. Stability is critical. Won't planting pathfinders all over the organization destroy stability?

The questions are easy. Let's now try for some answers.

Question 1: Do large organizations need pathfinding more now than they did in the past?

The answer to that question can be rather easily finessed by offering a collection of almost cliché observations. Here are some of them:

- In this ever smaller world, competition is getting stiffer. To beat out competitors with lower labor costs, one needs the compensating advantages of innovativeness and flexibility.

- In an ever more regulated environment, all organizations become more and more alike. Creativity and experimentation provide a pathway toward differentiating us from the pack, thereby giving us a comparative advantage over the rest.

- The birthrate of organizations is very high, and despite a high death rate, the organizational population keeps growing. In this crowded world, every decision we make immediately bumps us into somebody else's interests. It's easy to get stuck in a horrendous legal and competitive traffic jam. We need vision and determination to make our way through such crowded thoroughfares.

- Our modern work force brings high expectations with it. People in today's world want and expect much more than decent treatment and television sets. They want freedom; they want challenge; they want to take a few small steps for humankind. Tightly constrained organizational styles won't attract the good people.

- Even if the incredible rise of information technology doesn't in itself require more pathfinders, it provides a closely related challenge to managers. In large organizations, senior managers now hold (or soon will) the power to make more and more decisions—even day-to-day operational decisions—from the top. They can thereby reduce the autonomy of lower-level managers, using all that information to make the decisions themselves; or they can encourage pathfinding behavior by making sure that information is widely distributed for imaginative use everywhere. Which way they will go is still not clear, but if they try to grab all the power they can, pathfinding at lower levels will be in even shorter supply than it is now.

- As to the internal structure of organizations, most observers point to a broad trend toward looser, more fluid, less rigid organizational designs, and a major reason seems to be a felt need for more innovation. That trend is reflected in such books as Kidder's *Soul of a New Machine*,[1] which details the hectic, energetic, conflictful birth of a new computer, and Grove's *High Output Management*,[2] a CEO's description of Intel's open style and structure.

- Related to the trend toward more open, less hierarchical organizational structures is the trend toward *incrementalism* in both corporate and individual strategies—a shift toward flexibility and responsiveness, away from rigid plans and timetables. Indeed, the whole concept of corporate strategy, so popular in the 70s, is undergoing an agonizing reassessment. Much of the recent literature on corporate strategy argues for more incremental methods. Part of the rationale is that today's world is so complex and dynamic that fixed strategies (what Lindblom[3] long ago called "root strategies") are seldom appropriate. "Muddling through" strategies are often both necessary and effective. We do not need analytically derived formulas. We need to figure out where we want to go, the newer argument runs, and then take small steps in that general direction, cutting and trying and reassessing along the way. Such descriptive pieces as Kotter's *General Managers*,[4] Pascale's "Perspectives on Strategy,"[5] and Quinn's *Strategies for Change*[6] (subtitled *Logical Incrementalism*) carry the message of flexibility and incrementalism. But those incremental methods presuppose known and desired #1 direction, to guide the cut-and-try process. We need first to know in what general direction we are trying to go, in order to decide whether or not we have moved a bit that way today.

Except for one more item, that list must serve as an affirmative #2-type answer to question 1. We do need more pathfinding in organizations today. The additional item is a #1- rather than a #2-type item that the reader can delete at will: We need more pathfinding today because pathfinding is part of what I (the reader) believe our organizations just plain ought to be doing. It is, one might say, the duty of organizations to imagine and to innovate. And they haven't been doing very much of that lately.

Question 2: In the modern organization, is there room for pathfinders anywhere except at the top?

Back in the 18th century the word *company* (as, for example in the Hudson's Bay Company) meant a company of adventurers, of risk takers out to explore, develop, and create. The word still carries some of that meaning when it is used, say, for a company of actors or a dance company. It's time for the modern private sector business company to build some of that flavor back in. We need to form some venturesome companies of men and women within our larger corporate structures. The reasons are both numerous and obvious.

Large complex organizations simply cannot afford to isolate pathfinding as the special province of a small set of people. These days no CEO, even the brilliant founder, and no R&D group can generate all of the adventurous explorations, large and small, that organizations need to maintain their vitality.

In our fast-changing world, when *obsolete* refers to last month's product, there had better be plenty of room for pathfinders all over the organization. Unless we hold to an unlikely faith that our chairman's genius can encompass all that needs to be encompassed, innovations and experiments will have to come from the many instead of the few. And since failure rates for new ventures are probably going to stay high, a lot of fires will have to be started to find those few that will light up the sky.

Isolating pathfinding at the top may have been defensible in the past, but such vertical differentiation makes very little sense in modern organizations. It's an extremely inefficient way to use the sophisticated human talent that we now work so hard to recruit. Certainly some roles in the organization will continue to call for large portions of implementing behavior (for example, selling or line manufacturing) and others will continue to require mostly analytic problem solving (for example, financial accounting or corporate planning). But even *within* such roles, more elbowroom to allow innovative, entrepreneurial pathfinding can make the difference between creative, leading-edge development and slogging repetition of past routines.

There is still another way to look at it. You can't kill pathfinding propensities in human beings even if you want to. If any of us were to be so foolish as to try to prevent an organization's members from generating ideas and inventing clever ways of implementing them, we would find (as we have with computer hackers) that we had simply challenged them to even greater creativity, targeted at us. Forward-moving imagination, belief, and determination are as natural to humans as hunger and thirst. And yet many senior managers will complain about the absence of just these attributes in their people. In every case I have seen, however, the creativity is not absent; it is just tucked out of sight. It is usually hard to locate, either because sometime earlier the more daring people have departed, having found the organization a spiritual swamp, or because people are using their creativity underground, to fight or evade the system.

Question 3: Don't strong pathfinders at the top discourage pathfinding behavior elsewhere in their organizations?

Yes, they often do; but not always. From the brilliant

parent to the charismatic prime minister, great leaders often exert much more influence than even they intend to. Strong, persuasive parent figures can easily and unintentionally generate overdependency in their followers. "Our leader knows best." "Our leader will get us through this crisis." "Our leader will show us what to do." Like patients who *want* the doctor to know what's wrong, whether he really knows or not, followers often demand that their leaders make all of the key decisions. And since some leaders, like some physicians, enjoy that godlike role, they exacerbate the situation by magnanimously acceding to those pleas, thereby generating even more dependency.

I know one company founder who viewed himself that way, as the savior of his helpless flock. He saw his function as one of leading them—and the "them" in this case consisted of old war buddies and family members—into wealth and security. He wanted to lead them because he believed that they could not lead themselves. They needed him. He evoked loyalty and commitment from his people, but he evoked very little independence or imagination. When he finally went down, his whole flock went down with him.

It doesn't have to happen that way. Charismatic, pathfinding leaders can act as models for independent behavior instead of substitutes for it. They can encourage others to take risks, to initiate projects. Some contemporary organizations seem to be trying hard to do just that. Apple Computer is an interesting current example. Its founders—Jobs and Wozniak—were clearly #1 pathfinding types, and its leadership group tried hard to build up the spirited, wide-open, innovative atmosphere that they started; encouraging individual risk taking and inventiveness even as they tried to cope with growth, competition and shrinking markets. They established "Apple University," which was intended not primarily to dispense knowledge, but rather to inculcate the desired culture of inventiveness and exploration. Not surprisingly, Apple University's curriculum was consistent with that goal, even if it sometimes seemed a bit far-out to more conservative observers. It included exercises on survival in hard environments, challenging physical tasks, and courses on creative thinking.

Strong, visionary leadership need not discourage a general pathfinding style. That fact is illustrated best of all by our own American history. The clear and visionary leadership of the Founding Fathers of the United States, and the structure they designed to implement their vision, certainly did not cause either self-subordination among the American citizenry or undue reliance on higher authority. Quite the opposite. Their model required widespread independence, self-reliance, and innovation if it was to work successfully; and all things considered, it has worked pretty well.

The challenge for strong pathfinding leaders arises in the way they choose to play out the implementing part of their roles. When one has struggled for freedom, it is easy to revel in its achievement. Strong pathfinding leaders often take understandable pleasure, whether conscious of it or not, in their ability to control all aspects of their domains. It takes hard work, very hard yet passive work, to permit independence and initiative in others when that means reining in one's own autonomy—standing by, tolerating foolishness, and patiently permitting people to make their own mistakes. Organizations must restrict some of the freedoms of their leaders to enhance the freedom of everyone else.

Question 4: If everybody in a company becomes a pathfinder, how does the organization's work ever get done? Or, more bluntly, how the hell does anyone manage a whole stable full of pathfinding prima donnas?

It's not easy. On the face of it, the idea of "everyone a pathfinder" is about as far as one can get from the usual idea of a well-oiled, tightly coordinated organization. But we don't have to search very far to find certain classes of organizations that lean in the direction of "everyone a pathfinder"—even if they don't always lean that way by choice.

For a starter, talk to the local university president. He or she will regale you with the pains and tribulations of trying to manage a motley collection of independent faculty members. But when those presidents finish singing the blues, ask them what kind of people they're trying to recruit to add to that faculty. Answer: More prima donnas. And ask, "How do you manage such people?" And the answer will very often be something like: "I don't, at least I don't manage them very much. They manage themselves, more or less. I just try to raise money to support them and pay their computer bills." "How do you know they're doing good work?" "Their peers let them (and me) know if their work is below standard." "Don't they get into fights with one another?" "Constantly. It helps them think." "What about the teaching part of their jobs?" "Mostly they do it responsibly. Some complain about it. Some love teaching, and believe deeply in its importance; others see it as a necessary burden that distracts them from their research."

But universities are special kinds of organizations. They are there to teach, to do research, to seek truth. Pathfinding is their major function. My company just peels potatoes.

Of course, the modern university is not by any means an ideal model for business managers to emulate. It is only an illustration of a class of organizations that, by reason of tradition and function, leans in the pathfinding direction and still survive.

The local repertory theater provides a different kind of example of what's involved in managing collections of #1 individualists. Such organizations also seem to suffer frequent episodes of great stress and strain, but they usually hold together long enough to carry out their periodic common mission. Or ask the nearest pro football coach what it's like to manage his particular collection of individualists. It's tough. Pro football coaches usually don't last very long.

Companies aren't very different, are they? Senior engineers have told me that managing large software projects is a bit like managing a troupe of actors. Software types, they say, are undisciplined artists, each doing his own thing in his own way. They find that achieving coordination among them is horrendously difficult; but they muddle through.

Whether all or some professors, actors, athletes, and software specialists are pathfinding types or not, they tend toward individualism and autonomy. But they also all do some coordinated work inside an organizational tent. So part of the answer to question 4 is affirmative. Organizations *can* manage collections of individualists. Many of those organizations do it all the time.

But that doesn't tell us exactly *how* to manage such independent folk. Perhaps the most important suggestion that can be made about managing collections of autonomous people is to manage only at the absolutely critical points, letting intrinsic motivation, peer pressure, and personal integrity take care of most of the rest. Support, applause, reward—all of these will help; but formalizing, controlling, and nitpicking are much more likely to hurt.

Besides, a manager who staffed the whole company (or even a large chunk of it) with nothing but dedicated, all-out #1 pathfinders would be a damn fool. A manager who staffed it with nothing but #2 analysts would also be a damn fool. Imagine what managing that kind of organization would be like! And it would be just as dumb to staff the company with a single variety of #3 implementers. If they were political, manipulative #3s, you'd have to keep your backside carefully covered. Life would be one long game of power politics. If they were all participative, humanistic #3s, life might become one endless and intensive sensitivity group.

Prudence is appropriate. Adding more #1 spirit into the organization may be very much in order, but that doesn't mean flipping over into a brand-new organizational lifestyle.

We can surely make enough room in the modern organization to permit, indeed to encourage, *every* member to take a modest #1 stance—to initiate, to push for things that he or she believes in—while at the same time expecting those people to do the #2 and #3 parts of their jobs.

Question 5: What about the connection between #1 pathfinding and #3 implementing?

It won't be easy to bring them together. It will take some doing before they learn to love each other, but many organizations ought to be trying, over the next few years, to broker that potentially productive marriage.

What are the difficulties?

On the one hand, #1 pathfinding encourages individual managers to take proactive postures, to build clear missions and to communicate and inculcate those missions throughout the organization. That means active, energetic, purposive leadership. On the other hand, the contemporary #3 trend continues on the road toward participative and contingent forms of managerial leadership, sensitive but unobtrusive, egalitarian, and consensus seeking.

From the 1960s to the early 1980s, the most influential theories of managerial leadership were (*a*) participative theories and (*b*) contingent theories. Both are rooted in #3-type thinking. Both leave little room for charismatic and purposive individual leaders. The participative models focus on organizational process rather than purpose. They are concerned much more with finding paths to agreement and mutual trust than with finding paths to achievement. The closely related contingent models treat leadership reactively, urging managers to use specifically different behavioral styles for different situations. Both types of theories have considerable merit; but they have simply not concerned themselves with the pathfinding part of the managing process.

If we teach young managers only the principles of participative leadership, they will learn to equate leadership with listening to their people, building morale, patiently encouraging consensus. Is it also possible to teach them to be clear and firm in their purposes, to act as proactive and persuasive champions of their own views? And how do we teach young managers that they should encourage their people, in turn, to be firm in *their* purposes and to champion *their* beliefs?

If we teach them only contingent models, they will try to diagnose each set of situational conditions, and then to behave accordingly. If conditions X, Y, and Z exist, they must behave according to rule 3B. In both of the two cases, managers' behavior will be directed much more from without than from within.

There are some possible, though difficult, routes through these apparent dilemmas. Some of the alternatives receive more thorough consideration in a later chapter. For now, it is useful to point to two general approaches to the #1-#3 relationship.

The first approach is both the most common and the least satisfactory. It is to specialize and separate the two activities. The separation can be of a vertical type or a horizontal type. In the vertical type, the top managers take on the #1 pathfinding leadership and leave the participative/contingent activities to lower levels. That "solution" is likely to work only as long as those top managers are in place. It is also likely, in the longer term, to develop a dependent and passive work force. It is only as good and as durable as this generation of top managers.

The horizontal separation is even worse: Let the human resources staff people ply their participative/contingent trade through lower levels of the organization, and allocate the pathfinding duties to an internal new venture group or to the R&D division, or reserve those duties, as in the vertical model, to the chairman and the executive committee. That "solution" guarantees disastrous communication problems and destructive intergroup conflicts.

For a solution to the #1-#3 problem to have a chance, it had better be a systemic solution. We might call it "parallel and plural pathfinding." It has to integrate pathfinding with participative implementing throughout the organization. Everyone, everywhere has, to some degree, to play both leader and follower. The organization has to find ways to blend—as smoothly as possible—individualism and groupism throughout its domain, even within small organizational units. Organizations need both qualities, the sparkle and vitality of individualistic pathfinding styles and the coordination and teamwork of #3 styles.

One route to an effective plural and parallel union between pathfinding and participation is to build an organizational culture that welcomes both styles: a culture that puts high positive value on *both* pathfinding individualism and cooperative implementing. Once again a proximate example of such a mixed form is American culture itself. Our children have been taught for generations to be independent individualists and also collaborative team players. The prevalent stereotype of the aggressive, ambitious, confident American also includes, doesn't it, a good measure of cooperativeness, reliability, and capacity for teamwork? In its own rather chaotic way, that seemingly schizophrenic mix has had its ups and downs, but it has generally worked rather well, except when we have chosen to downplay one of the pair.

The fact that American society at large values both #1 and #3 styles is important to the manager. First, it means that only a short distance needs to be traveled to cross from the parent culture to a #1–#3 parallel pathfinding organizational culture. That short distance is a great blessing. For if an organization tries to build a culture that is extremely different from its surrounding parental culture, trouble is a certainty. The parent society will perceive the offending organization as an illegitimate enemy, and either imprison it with restrictive legislation and social pressures, or deport it, or kill it altogether. Moreover, recruits from that society will need serious remodeling to live in the new and different organizational culture. But if society at large has already inculcated those mixed values into its young people, organizations trying to recruit new members into a *similar* culture will find that much of their work has already been done for them.

Indeed, such a mixed, parallel, and plural culture is probably far easier to build into an American company than are the pure #3-type participative cultures that some of us have been trying to build. In fact, many of the tribulations of participative #3 methods in U.S. organizations can be attributed to trying to get people to jump too large a gap. Participative #3 techniques, like T-groups, transactional analysis, managerial grids, and team building, have frequently run into heavy flak in U.S. companies. Even when they succeed in becoming dominant styles for a while, they often wash out after a few years. One reason is that they are not fully consistent with the #1 side of American culture, though they are quite consistent with the #3 side. The independent part of the American personality sees such groupy methods as frustratingly conformist, un-American in their constraints on individualism.

In Japan and in Scandinavia, #3 methods have been adopted much more broadly and smoothly. In both of those parts of the world, #3 values are very deeply rooted in the larger cultures. But the traditions of Japan and Scandinavia do not include nearly as strong an emphasis on individualistic achievement as do those of the United States. The Japanese even treat such individualism as a sort of social evil, teaching their children *not* to evince personal ambition or to assert their individuality. An American anthropologist once observed that American parents punish their children by keeping them *in* the house, denying them independence and autonomy. Japanese parents keep them *out*, denying them membership in the family group.

A blend of #1 and #3 within individuals may therefore be easier to achieve in the American milieu than in some others, and easier to achieve than either #1 or #3 alone. While it may still look as though the mix requires a mildly schizophrenic, self-contradictory internal set of values, that isn't necessarily so. Instead of simply stirring #1 and #3 together by preaching and reinforcing both kinds of behavior, they can be blended in more careful and coherent ways. If, for example, we encourage teamwork but also try to build team norms and values that appreciate individualistic behavior by team members, perhaps we can get a bit of the best of both worlds. Must good groups, good teams, or effective task forces, by definition, reject members with deviant and unusual individualistic styles? Or, put the other way, what kinds and amounts of conformity must effective groups demand from their members? One possible format is insistence on conformity to a few key values, and only to those, while still leaving plenty of space for the unusual individual.

And if we kick the unit of analysis up a level to look at the relationship between the whole organization and the many groups within it, the same combination might work: a few inviolable commandments but plenty of room for the unusual group and the unusual individual.

Question 6: How about the #1 pathfinders versus the #2 problem solvers? How can we efficiently carry out the organizing, planning, and controlling #2 parts of the managing process and at the same time build dynamic, creative, determinedly independent #1 behavior within our organization?

I know one company founder whose central motivation was to build an organization that was *not* a bureaucratic slave state. Earlier, he had worked as a technologist in a large hierarchical company. He had felt so imprisoned there, so constrained by "all that bullshit," that, driven by a fervent dedication to freedom and autonomy, he started his own company.

When I first met him, he was looking for his fifth controller in two years. None of his controllers had worked out, because they all demanded too many Mickey Mouse reports and expense forms from his people. He needed a "creative controller," he said, one who could keep financial and tax data in order, but without laying on all of those bureaucratic regulations that kept his people from doing the interesting and important things. The major function of a good controller, he contended, was to help people, to relieve them of entangling paperwork, not to shackle them.

Not surprisingly, as his company has grown, that determined pathfinder has had to compromise some of his passion for individual freedom. For one thing, the company has to conform to governmental regulations, and as it grows, he himself needs better ways to keep his finger on its pulse. But despite the increasing pressures engendered by success, he continues to fight the good fight, and though his company's wide-open atmosphere has been compromised a bit, it remains a darn good breeding ground for technological pathfinders. Incidentally, one way he has kept the spirit alive has been by letting people set up their offices pretty much anywhere they want to. Physical distance can discourage those headquarters bean counters. Some people, of course, call the company a Turkish bazaar; but it's profitable and it's growing.

Any pathfinding founder, trying to maintain the pathfinding qualities of his growing organization, must inevitably find himself fighting a rearguard action—one that is laborious but not at all hopeless. As the organization grows (unless the founder chooses to keep it small), it will have to bow more and more to #2 pressures for order and control. If it doesn't accept more control, somebody down in the bowels of the company will violate regulations or screw up the specs of a contract or run afoul of the IRS. Then the whole company, not just the offending unit, will find itself enmeshed in enervating and unproductive trouble. In a regulated and litigious environment, every organization needs the skills and the styles of #2 tax lawyers, controllers, and accountants. We denigrate those specialists at our peril.

For reasons deep in the nature of human psychology and neurophysiology, #1 and #2 have a lot of trouble living together. The manager trying to promote synergistic integration between pathfinding and systematic planning and control is left with a very tough job. If we choose to simply stand by and let #1 and #2 fight it out, we can expect a fairly brief and one-sided war. Fragile, visionary #1 will be no match for #2's no-nonsense, short-term cost cutting and belt tightening. It's the #1 part that needs protection from those #2 bullies. Although society at large may support independent #1 behavior, organizations usually do not, for just the sorts of reasons that we have been discussing here—the need for good records, the pressures of regulation, the demands of stockholders and other investors. On the one hand, #1 ideas are often long term and nonprogrammable; they can be too readily delayed or put aside. On the other hand, #2 issues are both real and immediate: this quarter's budget, confronting the next directors' meeting, that cost overrun on the new equipment. Moreover, #1 ideas are frequently hard to support with good ROI data or with hard evidence of any kind. In a world that values tough-mindedness and thorough justification before it permits experimentation, #1 types often find themselves having to go underground if they want to dream unusual dreams.

Another challenging question was purposely omitted from our list. Can one build more #1 pathfinding into non-pathfinding *existing* organizations, with their *existing* people and *existing values*?

That too can and has been done, but we still don't know much about just how to do it. Academics haven't researched the problem very well. And managers haven't (until recently) experimented with it very much. They have both been too busy living in their #2 worlds. Nevertheless, that most important question deserves an exploratory chapter of its own—the next chapter.

Notes

[1] Tracy Kidder, *The Soul of a New Machine* (Boston: Little, Brown, 1981).

[2] Andrew Grove, *High Output Management* (New York: Random House, 1983).

[3] Charles E. Lindblom, "The Science of Muddling Through," *Public Administration Review* 19, no. 2 (1959). Reprinted in *Readings in Managerial Psychology*, 3d ed., eds. H. Leavitt, L. Pondy, and D. Boje (Chicago: University of Chicago Press, 1980).

[4] John D. Kotter, *The General Managers* (New York: Free Press, 1982).

[5] Richard T. Pascale, "Perspectives on Strategy," Stanford University Graduate School of Business Research Paper no. 686, 1982.

[6] James B. Quinn, *Strategies for Change: Logical Incrementalism* (Homewood Ill.: Richard D. Irwin, 1980).

BUILDING PATHFINDING INTO THE ORGANIZATION:
Small Steps toward Large Changes

In small young organizations pathfinding seems to come naturally. It is an organic part of their infancy and child-hood. We don't have to worry about injecting more path-finding spirit into such organizations. Indeed, investors in small start-up companies usually worry about the opposite question: How can we slow these guys down? Let's put a lawyer on the board! Let's get them to hire a hard-nosed controller! But larger, older organizations seldom show the urgency and excitement of the start-up company. By their third or fourth management generation, most organizations have lost much of that entrepreneurial pathfinding zeal, un-intentionally replacing it with the stolid, stable, and unin-spired routinization of middle age. Somehow, even while such organizations remain competent and successful, the bold pathfinding vitality often quietly shrivels away, its loss unnoticed amidst pressures for growth, control, and effi-ciency.

The purpose of this chapter is *not* to ask whether more pathfinding is or is not appropriate in any particular organi-zation. It is simply to offer a partial checklist of steps that managers might take if they choose to try to instill more pathfinding spirit into their existing organizations.

This chapter goes at that issue from three angles. It first looks at new, young organizations because they almost al-ways show such pathfinding spirit, trying to identify the attributes that distinguish them from other organizations. Then it asks how and why larger and older organizations so often lose those pathfinding attributes. And the third ap-proach is to list some concrete steps that should help to nudge larger, older organizations toward recapturing some youthful urgency and animation.

Let's try all three.

Why is it so exciting to be young?

Small young companies seem almost always to show an entrepreneurial, pathfinding spirit. Why? If we can answer that question, perhaps we can figure out how to transfer some of that spirit to their older and bigger siblings. Here are some characteristics of new, young organizations that are related to pathfinding zeal:

- Most small young organizations are quite *unspecialized* and *nonhierarchical*. They are nonbureaucratic, not formalized. Everybody pretty much does everything, without narrow job descriptions, without organization charts. The common task drives the system. There may be debate, argument, even recrimination, but the focus stays on what needs to be done.

  As the small company grows bigger, specialization and hierarchy begin to move in; and the totally consuming atmosphere of urgency and enthusiasm begins to move out.

- Small new organizations are also, because they have to be, *improvisational*. They are blessedly naive, ignorant of the ways of the world. Most of the situations they encounter are new to them. Uncertainty and crisis are the order of the day. So they improvise, they ad lib, they muddle through, working things out as they go. As some problems recur, again and again, that improvisational style gives way to more regular routines. Intelligent human beings are learners. If they've done it a couple of times, they read the cues and develop standardized responses. It's like ticktacktoe. The first few times you play, you experiment and explore. Once you've come to understand the game, you can play it out in a routine way. And at that point, the game becomes uninteresting.

- Small new organizations are typically *informal*. Discussion and argument go on endlessly at that stage, without much regard for status or title. Only later do we begin to go the #2 route, delineating and differentiating roles, establishing formal ranks and prescribed areas of responsibility. Proposition: Other things equal, an informal structure is more likely than a formal one to foster pathfinding behaviors.

- Small new organizations are usually *groupy*. They are, in fact, often started by three or four adventuresome colleagues who share a we-are-all-in-this-together fervor. They show some of the qualities of an infantry company in tough combat, viewing themselves as a kind of embattled enclave. Deep human feelings emerge from such togetherness in a common struggle—feelings of mutual trust and support, feelings bordering on love. Such feelings provide a sense of security even in insecure situations, a sense of membership, and a sense of personal worth—all of which enhance both creativity and determination. Success, and the growth that accompanies it, usually erode those feelings, often leaving frustration and rancor in their place.

- The mixture of groupiness and informality in small organizations, coupled with small physical size, enables *easy communication*. A setting that permits frequent and convenient face-to-face communication provides an ideal soil for shaping and sharing values and for developing mutual determination. With the physical separation and longer communication chains that accompany growth, such communication becomes more and more difficult, even with contemporary communication technology.

- Small new organizations are almost always led by intensely *dedicated leaders*. No matter how varied their personalities, the founder-leaders of such companies typically share a deep dedication to their organizations. The reasons are not mysterious. The founder-leaders are owners as well as managers, and owners usually show considerable interest in the things they own, particularly when they've mortgaged their worldly goods to gain that ownership. For most founder-owners of new companies, the company is the most central thing in their lives, the most important thing that has ever happened to them. Their necks are on the block.

    As those dedicated organizations grow up, a generation or two down the road, "professional" managers step in. In this context, "professional" means nonfounders, nonowners. The impassioned determination of the founders fades into the bland standoffishness of the cool professional manager. Promotions, career paths, stock options, and vacations then become central foci of managerial attention. For the founders, those words had no meaning whatsoever.

- Small new organizations usually have, or manage to create, clear and powerful *enemies*. The actual or imagined threat from those enemies stimulates enthusiasm and a sense of urgency, as well as feelings of togetherness. If big bad IBM is out there trying to stomp on us, or the American Medical Association or TWA or AT&T, then we know we just have to be better and brighter and more resolute than ever before. We have no time for selfish squabbling or internal power plays.

- Small new organizations are *fun*. Despite long hours and intensive work, people enjoy the early stages of a company's life. They are remembered as intimate, warm, happy times. The veterans of those start-up days almost always look back on them with nostalgia, as peak experiences in their lives. It doesn't seem to matter how laborious, frightening, and exhausting those times may in reality have been. Such climates of animation and commitment are difficult to maintain even in small organizations. In large ones, they often disappear altogether.

One way of targeting the characteristics of a pathfinding atmosphere, then, is to try to recreate, in one's mind's eye, the urgent, purposive climate of the start-up days of the small new organization. How does one build that vitality into the large old organization, with its set-in-their-ways middle managers, its formalistic hierarchy, its rigid union contracts, and its regulated environment? And more important, how does one maintain it over long periods of time?

Must older organizations lose their #1 yeast?

It's both sad and dangerous that so many organizations eventually reject their own pasts. Two or three decades after their founding, the once-heroic founders come to be seen as quaint, but irrelevant, old-fashioned characters, to be trotted out at the annual company picnic. How many of those founders would now be turned down by their own organization's recruiters because they are too "abrasive" or "stubborn" or "uncooperative"?

It is not just a matter of passively forgetting our organization's origins; we often actively reject the founders and their beliefs, as though we were ashamed of them. Just as many first-generation Americans, in their search for respectability, used to be ashamed of their parents' old country accents and habits, new generations of managers often prefer to depart as quickly as possible from their rough-hewn origins, dressing up instead in the three-piece costumes of "professionalism."

Must it happen that way? To some degree, yes. Experienced readers know that growth really does require us to give up some of the management-by-impulse so typical of eccentric founders—to show more discipline, to get ourselves organized, to define structures and tighten controls. With more people and more space, more hierarchy is just about inevitable. Some of the formalization is indeed a bid for respectability. Professional managers, after all, want to show off their organization charts and job descriptions and incentive schemes as well as their striped ties. But hierarchy and formalization are not just devices to enhance legitimacy and power. Hierarchy permits efficient implementation of complex tasks. Subassembling, departmentalizing, and specializing all make sense, especially for complicated tasks requiring the work of large numbers of people and spread out over large geographic areas. As organizations grow, more formal communication and control systems make sense too. The many parts of the organization need more systematic ways of knowing what the other parts are doing. When will subassembly A be ready for installation by group B? What has been built or sold or ordered, and when?

While the establishment of clear and stable structures in large organizations is a sensible way to meet an obvious need, it can also be very destructive of pathfinding climates. Should any of us, for example, be much surprised by the following item from the front page of the *New York Times* of April 21, 1985?

In a confidential Army survey of its officer corps, taken last fall and analyzed over the winter, half the officers who answered a long questionnaire agreed that the bold, original, creative officer cannot survive in today's Army. . . . 68 percent agreed that the officer corps is focused on personal gain rather than selflessness.

It does not seem very surprising that officers feel that way in "today's Army." Is there any reason to believe that they felt differently in yesterday's? It will be a far-off day indeed when half of its officers can say that an organization of the size, tradition, and function of the U.S. Army has become a place where "the bold, original, creative officer" *can* survive.

Formal structures depersonalize organizations. From a company of unique individual human beings, we convert to a company of jobs and roles into which people can be, more or less interchangeably, plugged. Formalization drives toward routinization and repetition. It kills excitement and encourages territoriality. It generates game playing to make people look good on the parameters that are evaluated, and often to neglect those that are not. It causes more and more separation of #2 staff types (usually housed at headquarters) from #3 implementers. So movement from plans to actions becomes a more laborious and often adversarial process accompanied by a diversion of energy away from the work itself and toward between-group conflicts.

More and more demand for rational justification of proposals almost always accompanies such formalization. Transfer pricing becomes a hassle. Who sets the price you are to pay me for the parts my unit makes to be installed in the widget that your unit assembles and sells? If the price is low, your unit looks good and my unit shows very little profit. If it's high, my unit looks great and yours looks terrible. Books of standard rules and procedures grow thick. "A din of reasons" (to use Chester Barnard's phrase) must now accompany every proposal, dampening, albeit inadvertently, the excitement and spontaneity associated with innovative and venturesome ideas. The "let's try it" attitude of the small new organization is supplanted by the paper chase of the bureaucracy.

More infighting usually follows, helped along by more formal performance evaluations. Individuals perceive other individuals—and groups perceive other groups—as competitors or enemies. We marketing people have to fight like hell because those engineers are trying to dominate this company. And I have to fight like hell to beat that lowlife who will do anything to get that promotion. Sometimes such conflicts energize pathfinding. Most of the time they just energize gamesmanship.

Much more oversight becomes necessary to make sure that legal and regulatory requirements are met. Hence tighter controls are established on contract specifications, hiring practices, safety, product characteristics, meetings with competitors, and on and on. Such shackling requirements are not conducive to innovative experimentation, creative dreams, or imaginative visions.

Neurotic needs to maintain power at the top of the organization frequently intrude themselves as companies grow. "It's my show," says the top manager. "I'm responsible for making it work. My bonus depends on it, and so does my reputation. So I will make the decisions around here." And the more difficult the times, the greater is the propensity to concentrate decision making at the top.

In large old organizations, concerns about the trappings of power can be as debilitating as grabbing for real power, draining energy away from the organization's central mission. As companies grow large and successful, they erect great stone edifices to memorialize imperial CEOs. The offices of the powerful always seem to migrate to the top floor; and those offices must be silent, awe-inspiring, and lavishly underdecorated. Limos and private dining rooms are appended, along with a hierarchy of other perks: company cars, club memberships, keys to the executive washroom. All of these in turn become visible but task-irrelevant indicators of personal progress to which lower-level personnel now aspire. Young idealists are thus seduced away from their ideals, and the straightforward, task-directed objectives of earlier times are supplanted by funless games.

When the organization is young and struggling, new employees can see themselves joining a social movement, a cause. Mere membership in the organization carries a value of its own. The organization embodies something to identify with, something to love. In large old organizations, new employees don't usually think of themselves as volunteers in a great and valuable crusade; they're just taking a job. Nor are senior executives much different. They too are more likely to look for better jobs, not for more inspiring causes. And when they get that better job, they then work hard to impress the board with their energetic cost cutting. There is less dedication here—and less passion. Maturity usually moves organizations away from urgency and emotionality and toward a cooler, more orderly, and more systematic appearance, an appearance that only thinly covers the Sturm und Drang that lie beneath it.

In such large, hierarchical organizations, senior executives frequently complain that their juniors are not creative or entrepreneurial or "risk taking." Those complaints seem a little hollow. Long chains of communication, elaborate multilevel evaluation procedures, insistence on extensive justifications for proposals—all of those would discourage even the most dedicated pathfinder. After a few tries at getting our boss to talk to his boss, who sends it to the legal department before it can go to the new products evaluation committee, which won't meet again until next February— after all of that, even pathfinding types are likely either to quit trying or to quit the company.

OK already, says the frustrated reader, I've heard that harangue before. But large organizations have to behave that way. We need controls; we need evaluation procedures; we need to make choices; we need to allocate our scarce resources carefully. And remember, it's the stockholders' money we're guarding. So what if some people can't do everything they want to do in such a setting? That's just the way it is. It's one of the bills we have to pay for the productive power of the large organization.

Up to a point, that's a fair and sensible argument. It doesn't, however, justify those complaints about our people's lethargy and lack of initiative. If it's initiative we want, and if it's the organization's structure and control systems that block it, the way to go is to encourage people to behave like people. And the way to do that is to loosen up that structure and those controls to give people more elbowroom. Then, if nothing happens, such complaints will warrant more serious consideration.

Some #2-type advice on building a #1 climate into the large organization

Can we make a list of specific procedures that will help to build and maintain a #1 spirit inside even a large #2-type formalized structure?

Here are some possibilities:

1. Let's start with a common but very bad idea. Separate and specialize #1 pathfinding activities from #2 problem solving activities and from #3 implementing activities. We mentioned earlier the CEO who argued that his company had, he felt, solved the problem that way. Lower-level people were given #3 implementing jobs: selling, bench engineering, production jobs, and the like. Middle-level people took over the #2 planning and organizing jobs. The #1 jobs became the exclusive territory of top management. They would do the imagining and the mission setting.

That simple solution, unfortunately, occurs quite commonly in larger, older organizations. It never works. That three-step scheme not only fails to solve the problem but almost always exacerbates it. Defining #1 as the domain of top management signals the middle and bottom that they are *not* to create or imagine or champion. That's not their job.

In today's world of bright, highly educated employees, that three-step scheme also means that the #1 ball is given to those who may not be the most capable of carrying it—the older, more jaded players. Moreover, asking the young to delay their dreams and store away their ideals until they reach the top guarantees that those dreams and ideals will either wither away or that the young will try some other place where they might have a better shot at fulfilling them sooner. "Be thrifty when you're young," a cynical old saying goes, "so that when you're old, you'll be able to afford the things that only the young can enjoy."

2. A more sensible #2-type proposal is to try to stimulate innovation through rewards and incentive systems. Paying positive attention to the #1 area by offering rewards for inventions, for projects carried through, for suggestions, is both an old idea and a modern one. Companies have been fiddling with money incentives for more than a hundred years, trying everything from piece rates to executive bo-

nuses. Often rewards and incentives have had very salutary effects, but occasionally they bomb out.

In their modern forms, experiments with incentives have been mushrooming again in Western companies. There is one big difference, however, between the old experiments and the new ones. The new ones try to reward #1 behavior, while most of the old ones tried to stimulate only #3 implementation. Many of the newer schemes provide incentives for innovativeness as distinct from productivity, and for pioneering effort as distinct from successful results. The newer schemes may also pay off in currencies other than cash. Some offer a percentage of royalties or license fees or a chance to participate in setting up and running the new venture that may be spawned from a new idea. Some offer nonmonetary rewards—sabbaticals, fellowships, or other opportunities to do what one wants to do for some period of time. Even entirely symbolic incentives have been offered, as Intel's use of M & M candies to reward individual contributors.

It is clear that many benefits can derive from such incentive plans. When people know they will be rewarded if they make something important happen, they are certainly more likely to try. But such offers of the pot of gold had better be accompanied by the necessary peripherals: time and space, so that there is a real chance to work on that hot idea, and a general atmosphere that encourages the venturesome. In some companies, for example, R&D people are allowed 10 or 15 percent of undirected time for independent explorations of their own choice. If that opportunity is backed up with modest resources and convenient channels for presentation, some positive #1 outcomes are very likely to follow. It's curious that such things are almost never done in accounting departments, or in manufacturing.

There are serious potential dangers in these modern incentive schemes, even as there were in earlier ones. In the old days of piece rates, "rate-busters" were frequently ostracized by their peers and the fixing of piece rates caused endless bickering between company and unions. The newer incentive plans, applied mostly to knowledge workers, can also backfire, leading to competitive secrecy (I'll hide my great idea so no one will steal it until I win the prize), debates about ownership (Did he really deserve that whole reward? Didn't she make a significant contribution?), and other kinds of nonproductive interpersonal and intergroup resentment.

Like most powerful tools, incentives can cut both ways. They can stimulate and support a climate of creative urgency, or they can increase tension, feelings of injustice, and dishonest communication. Which way they go depends heavily on the background culture into which they are embedded. Tossed carelessly into an environment of low trust, adversarial postures, and competitive factions, new incentives will not eliminate those problems. Instead they will be quickly absorbed into the existing scene to exacerbate them. Remember Atari, the computer game company that produced Pac-Man and many more? In 1981 and 1982 that company was one of the hottest in Silicon Valley. In 1976, when it was sold by its founder to Warner Communications, its annual sales had reached $2 billion. Then the market fell apart. A story entitled "What Went Wrong at Atari," which appeared in the *San Jose Mercury News* of November 6, 1983, describes one of the incentive plans that blew up. The then CEO of Atari had already lost a key set of VCS programmers.

In February 1982, when another group of VCS programmers threatened to leave, Kassar [the CEO] panicked. If they quit, Atari would have no VCS programmers left. . . . He responded by throwing money at the designers. Salaries were increased and a hastily-created bonus plan was instituted.

But because the bonus plan rewarded sales and not quality or originality, it created more problems than it solved. The big question became "Who gets to do the hot coin-op and movie ti-

tles?" *Tod Frye, who did the Pac-Man conversion, earned between $1 and $1.2 million for his efforts. The other designers felt any one of them could have done it. They became secretive, not talking to each other or to marketing people because they did not want to share their royalties. When the company brought in a New York compensation analyst to find out why the designers weren't producing, the analyst called them "the wealthiest, most unhappy group of people I've ever met."*

*"What's amazing is that all that money didn't get people to be more productive," Kaplan [the compensation analyst] says. "Programmers just sat around worrying about how to get more money. They'd approach a project with a 'how much am I gonna make off this game?' attitude."**

However, when incentives are added to a more positive culture, with a clear sense of mission and a high level of trust, they can indeed help spread a pathfinding atmosphere throughout the company.

3. Try increasing "time spans of discretion" everywhere in the organization. The time span of discretion (a concept developed by Eliot Jaques) is the length of time between inspections, or controls, or evaluations. That time span has traditionally been very short for closely supervised blue-collar or clerical jobs, with longer and longer time spans accompanying higher-level jobs. While an assembly line worker may have to live within a 50-second span, senior managers may work with quarterly or even annual spans.

Pathfinding climates have to provide quite long time spans of discretion, time to explore and experiment. So one way to enable more pathfinding in the large organization is to extend those periods of discretion everywhere. That may not entail changes in the nature of the standard controls or evaluations, only in the frequency of their application.

Unfortunately, it is not just the formal controls that are

---

* What Went Wrong with Atari, *San Jose Mercury News Magazine*, November 6, 1983.

important here, but also the informal ones—the implicit expectations about when we should be in our offices, what the "normal" length of lunch hours is, when we must look busy, which meetings we must be seen at. Those implicit limits on our discretion can be much more difficult to change than the explicit ones. There is, of course, a serious cost involved in abandoning such informal norms. They serve important unifying functions. So the trick in most cases is to loosen up those norms without destroying them altogether.

In a similar vein, it is also useful to look for means of opening up physical and psychological space. Can we, even in large organizations, find ways of giving our people more space? It's not larger offices that are at issue here but more freedom to move around the organization and in and out of it—to cross divisional boundaries or hierarchical levels. Pathfinding is more likely when people don't always have to stick close to their specialized jobs and when they can easily talk to people who are not immediate colleagues. Why? Because specialists in one skill can often offer fresh insights into specialties quite distinct from their own and because their own specialties may be enhanced by ideas from elsewhere.

4. One way to encourage innovation is to *specialize* it— for example, by setting up an innovation department, as in the R part of the R&D division. Such groups, of course, are typically targeted only at the technological side of the business, at process or product improvement. We don't usually do much of our own internal R&D in a search for better control systems, or organizational designs, or alternative organizational cultures.

New venture groups and task forces are two other currently popular methods for specializing some aspects of pathfinding. But they are very different from each other. The new venture group is usually a formal, ongoing division within the existing organizational structure, charged with searching out new markets, new products, or new ventures.

The task force, which has also become a widely used tool for pathfinding in recent years, is another kettle of fish. IBM (for its PC), Apple (for its Macintosh), and many other companies have used task forces effectively in developing new products. Carefully selected (often self-selected) groups, their members dedicated to a specific purpose, are set out by themselves under the leadership of a determined champion and given lots of temporal, spatial, and behavioral discretion.

While they may look alike, new venture departments and those small task forces are not relatives. The key difference is in the source from which they spring. New venture departments usually emerge as #2-type formally planned add-ons to existing hierarchical structures. They are set up for problem finding—to go hunting, systematically, for new opportunities. They are cool, and they are permanent. Task forces—the ones that really seem to work—typically emerge much more spontaneously from ideas that excite people. They are hot, and they are temporary. They are driven by some challenging vision, some mission that has stirred the blood. New venture groups often exert very little influence on the rest of the organization's style, while internal task forces, highly visible, are more likely to be read as significant indicators of the general organizational style.

5. Another extremely powerful and quite old-fashioned way to bring more pathfinding into organizations is personnel selection. What kind of people shall we invite into our organization? Do we actively search for pathfinder types? When IBM's Mr. Watson, Jr. took over the company he was, it seems, worried about the conformity and discipline that then pervaded the organization, so he called for a search for more "wild ducks," a phrase that later came into wide usage in the company. Could we identify such people even if we wanted to? Or do we go for more solid recruits—competent, steady, well-trained citizens? Or should consideration for

getting along with people become our primary criterion for selection? What is our definition of an excellent recruit?

Initial selection may not look important, because a large organization will sooner or later either socialize recruits into its ways of doing things, or it will eject them. They will shape up or ship out. But that argument is naive. It ignores the other face of that coin. While it's true that organizations change people, it's equally true that people change organizations. The kinds of people we bring into the company will leave their marks on the company's existing culture even as they are being acculturated into it. A steady inflow of new people, with new ways of thinking, will slowly but surely nudge even a huge organization toward change.

In recent years, for technical and white-collar jobs, we have tried to select mostly for #2 skills. That is fairly easy because records of academic success and test scores provide reasonably satisfactory metrics. For young engineers or financial analysts, good grades are a pretty good raw indicator of #2 competence. We have also put some less successful effort into identifying characteristics related to implementing, like psychological stability and sociability. Our selection criteria, however, have seldom tried to identify such #1 attributes as sense of purpose, or deep beliefs in particular values, or entrepreneurial flair. Indeed, if such purposive visionary qualities were noticed at all, they often got negative points from recruiters and admissions officers of business schools. They were seen as signs of nonmalleability or impracticality, if not downright maladjustment.

Graduate business schools, while presumably educating future leaders, have been among the worst offenders in that regard. We selected *smart* students (by test score standards) rather than dedicated ones. We also sought pliable students who, unclear about themselves, would accept what we had to teach. People who already knew what they wanted might not be so docile. We looked for high scores on the quantitative scale of the GMAT, not for imagination or resolve. The two-year education that followed selection only served to socialize students into even greater uniformity, even to the point of widespread consensus about which companies "good" students should try to work for. As a result, we got high-quality, first-class students, but they were not necessarily high-quality, first-class pathfinders.

Selection can unquestionably become a critical step in the search for pathfinding, but it is not an easy step. Again the existing structure dictates against changes in itself. To go after the occasional interesting oddball, the out-of-step type, is risky for recruiters' own careers. It's dangerous to be blamed for hiring weirdos, loners, and nerds, and that's the way some managers will see such unusual recruits. People like that will be irritants, disturbers of the peace. Besides, if they're hired but not supported by appropriate backup, they'll soon go away.

6. How about simply setting up in-house education and training programs to teach pathfinding skills? Yes, if (a) trainers are ready to do some serious work in designing such programs and (b) if what those programs teach is consonant with the company's style.

Training, if it consists of a short course in creative thinking, isn't going to be very effective in developing pathfinders. Further, if the training courses teach people to think more divergently and to champion their ideas, while the company goes right on demanding convergent thinking and passive obedience, the results, of course, will be counterproductive. And yet a wide gap between what is taught in management courses and what is practiced by the sponsoring organizations is not at all unusual.

Trainers in large companies are often unwilling to confront interesting but risky challenges. They, like the rest of us, usually choose to follow this year's fashion in new training programs. But developing more effective methods for teaching pathfinding skills and then supporting them in large organizations constitutes a real and major challenge for the next decade. It will take much imagination and determination to develop such methods, and even more to gain organizational support.

7. Job rotation is another good device for trying to build a little more pathfinding into the organization—not just for the usual reason of broadening the rotated employee's experience but because new people in old jobs often carry with them the insight of the innocent. They ask those good dumb questions that cause the rest of us to look again for the emperor's new clothes.

8. Physical design can play a significant role in either discouraging or encouraging a pathfinding climate. Color schemes, office layouts, grounds and gardens, and building designs are surely relevant, though the rules to tell us what's better or worse are not always clear. Apple Computer, in its dedication to exuberant and youthful openness, goes in for bright primary colors. Are those brilliant red and green and yellow offices any more conducive to innovative thinking than the dark, damp, and decaying walls of a 17-century palazzo in Venice?

Recently I met with a senior executive from a fast-growing and innovative young company who argued cogently against those huge steel and glass headquarters buildings so common to large companies everywhere. Even banks, he argued, would do better without their marble palaces and 30-foot ceilings. While those sturdy fortresses symbolize stability, he insisted, they also discourage flexibility, agility, and creativity. Given easy, fast travel and communication, and the whole world as the company's territory, his company preferred simple offices, with meetings of relevant people anywhere and anytime they were needed.

An even stronger argument can be made against the typical design of classrooms in business schools. They are usually amphitheaters, consisting of permanently fixed tiers of seats bolted behind long, curved writing surfaces. The rows descend to a central pit, where the lone faculty member is expected to stand in solitary splendor, there to Teach. Such classrooms partially define what education must be and what it must not be. They leave little room for experimenting with alternative kinds of teaching arrangements. They operationally and narrowly specify for the young teacher what teaching means, and for the young student, what learning means.

Physical design can also be intentionally used to dictate against pathfinding. I know one large privately held company, headquartered on many acres of hills, ponds, and trees and located in a climate ideal for outdoor lunches or walks or sports. But the rather authoritarian CEO does not permit employees to use those grounds. They can look at the trees through their office windows, and they can drive among them as they arrive and depart, but there are no tables or benches at which to eat their lunches alfresco. His reason is not ecological. He is quite consciously trying to assure tight discipline and obedience. He isn't interested in employee creativity. Work is work. Strolling in the woods, he believes, is not work. So far, the company is doing very well, but the atmosphere is rather subdued.

9. Pathfinding flowers seem to grow better in smaller, younger organizational units than in larger, older ones. It's difficult to make old organizations young again, but temporary and frequently rebuilt teams and task forces are always possible. And it's quite possible, in many cases, to downsize large units to smaller ones. So even large, old organizations can, with effort, reclaim some of the fertile characteristics of their lost youths.

Now that the reader has been given a list of tactics for enhancing the pathfinding flavor of an organization, it is time to offer a warning about their use. The danger is that lists of individual pieces don't always add up to wholes. Seats, handlebars, and wheels are not a bicycle; and task forces, incentive plans, and open offices don't, in themselves, constitute a pathfinding climate. Some integrating gestalt is needed to give coherence to the whole system. The next chapter takes a more holistic, more total-immersion approach to building coherent pathfinding corporate cultures into nonpathfinding organizations.

CHAPTER
8

FROM ORGANIZATIONAL
MISSION TO
ORGANIZATIONAL CULTURE:
Managing the Mist

If you want to know about a company's culture, take a seat at the local bar, just after working hours, with a few people from the company across the street. Ask them what it's like to work for that outfit. Their answers will give you a quick fix on that organization's culture. It will be only a partial picture of the culture, because much of what they think and feel about their company won't convert into words. But you'll get a pretty good idea, even through the limiting and distorting medium of words, about the atmosphere, the style, the "climate" of the company. You'll probably also get contradictions and inconsistencies too, but that's how cultures are. Nobody has ever succeeded very well in measuring the differences between, say, the contemporary French and British cultures, but anyone who has visited both countries, even for a few days, will swear that they are quite distinct, and will go on to detail purported differences in everything from drinking habits to attitudes toward children. Cultures have the ephemeral qualities of flame or fog. You know they're there; you know they're real; but you can't grab hold of them or even describe them very well.

This chapter tries to show how the pathfinding part of managing shapes organizational culture. The chapter has two major parts: First, it tries to pin down the concept of organizational culture just a bit. What is it? What isn't it? Second, it considers how organizational leaders can build and manage their organizations' cultures. Managers don't always build those cultures intentionally; and the cultures they actively build don't always turn out to be the ones they hoped for. But like it or not, and intend it or not, managers build cultures.

Organizational culture: Is it for real? And if it is, does it really matter?

Culture is an umbrella word. It refers to a whole package of implicit, frequently unconscious, widely shared beliefs, traditions, values, morals, expectations, and habits that characterize a particular group of people. Culture is to the organization what "personality" and "character" are to the individual. Like our personalities, our organizational cultures are usually more clearly visible to others than to ourselves. They're too much a part of us for us to see them very clearly. Like the character of individuals, the moral and ethical qualities of our organizational cultures are so deeply built in that we hardly notice they are there.

Cultures, organizational and otherwise, serve important functions for us. They are comforting; they are controlling; and they limit and direct our vision.

They comfort us with their familiarity. It's always somehow nice to be back home among our own people, and it's always a little anxiety provoking when we first enter an unfamiliar culture—a strange country or a new company. We are grateful, then, for guidance and "orientation." We also know that it will take a while to learn the ropes, to understand the signals, to pick up the special language of that culture. But once we have learned the ropes, our cultural surround becomes comforting and reassuring, even when we don't particularly love it.

Once we are members, once we belong, we look at other cultures differently. Remember a few years ago when some U.S. auto workers from Detroit went to visit and work at Volvo plants in Sweden? Volvo was using a sort of group-based production system, quite different from and a lot more "human" than the tight assembly lines of Detroit. When those line workers came home, almost all of them reported that they still liked our American way better. Volvo's style was OK for Swedes but not for Americans. This was taken by some observers as evidence that American workers preferred short work cycles and assembly lines over group-based systems. Was it really evidence of such preferences? Or was it perfectly predictable that whatever the differences, Americans would prefer their familiar, known, understood culture to a strange one?

Organizational cultures are not just comforting; they are also controlling. Our organizational cultures tell us that people here go to work at 8, not at 8:15, and leave at 6; that they write short memos; that women wear skirts, not pants; that we celebrate birthdays but not anniversaries; that we don't gossip about the boss; that we support our soccer team. In a thousand ways, many of them critically related to work, our organizational cultures serve as control systems, implicitly teaching us where the limits and the boundaries are. But cultures are front-end, built-in control systems—very different from the control systems we usually think about when we hear that phrase in organizations.

Cultures put blinders on their members. Because it's just the way things are, and perhaps also the way things have always been, we find it hard to see beyond our cultures, to other ways of thinking, feeling, or acting. We cannot imagine, even when we visit other cultures or see them on television, that we could live or behave like those Pygmies or those Eskimos or those Japanese managers.

We value our cultures. Our cultures' ways become the right ways. Not only do we not eat puppy dogs; we also find such behavior repugnant and uncivilized. What we do is not just what we do but what people ought to do. Cultures can thus become highly resistant to change. Indeed, the stronger the culture, the more widely shared and deeply held are its beliefs and practices and the harder it is to change.

So cultures, organizational and otherwise, are (1) real, (2) mostly taken for granted, (3) extremely controlling and directing of our behavior, and (4) very hard to change.

That organizational cultures are a real and relevant dimension of organizations means that managers had better try to manage them. That they are mostly taken for granted means that they are probably ripe for creative problem finding. If we pay more careful attention to them, we may be able to find interesting ways to use them. That they are controllers of their members' behavior means that they are potentially powerful tools for disciplining the organization. And that they are very hard to change means, among other things, that before we try to build new cultures, we should think twice about them. We may have to live with those cultures for a long time.

If all of that sounds a little too abstract, here's another way of thinking about the place of the culture in the larger managing process: What determines whether that new performance appraisal scheme will really work? Is it the characteristics of the scheme itself, the forms, the frequency of use, the skill of the users? Yes, but even more it's the fit of the new scheme into the existing culture. Given a culture that fears change and distrusts management's motives, the best of the new appraisal methods will be treated as just another gimmick to be avoided, outmaneuvered, or delayed. Are quality circles a good idea? Only if the larger culture finds them reasonable and acceptable. Is the new stock option plan a good one? No matter how clever it is from a financial and tax point of view, it won't fly if it violates the culture. Culture shapes the eye of the beholder.

I remember talking to the CEO of a small fabricating company who had magnanimously installed an air conditioning unit on his shop floor. He figured that more comfortable temperatures would make "even those bastards" work a little better. In fact, it produced the opposite results. In the adversarial atmosphere of that plant, even something as positive as air conditioning was rejected by the work force as another trick that "that SOB thought up to try to get us to work harder."

In the same vein, London's *Financial Times* of December 5, 1984, reported the following differences in perception between two subcultures—management's and the union's— within the same corporation:

Complaints from the white-collar union Apex took a bit of the shine off British Airways' new 42m corporate image yesterday. Training methods being used to instill staff loyalty and commitment to BA's new motto "To Fly To Serve" amounted to "brainwashing," the union claimed.

Assistant general secretary Keith Standring said that American industrial psychologists at BA training courses at Bristol *were: Putting pressure on people to go swimming and jogging each morning before breakfast; causing sensory deprivation for some staff who were walking about blindfolded for hours during role-play exercises; and forcing people to eat meals without a knife and fork. "The purpose," said Standring, calling for the courses to be scrapped, "is to create an atmosphere which makes people give total commitment to the airline." He had been informed that some staff had undergone dramatic personality changes during the courses. Back at Lord King's headquarters, a BA spokesman said that the whole thrust of the training courses was to improve service to BA's customers. "People have been asked to put on a blindfold to appreciate the problems of blind travellers," he said. "It is a voluntary exercise." Equally voluntarily, some had eaten chicken legs with their fingers and gone jogging to exercise their desk-bound legs. All a token, no doubt, of the energy, strength and vitality represented in BA's new coat of arms.**

It's through such distorting cultural mists that the members of organizations interpret the concrete actions that take place around them. While actions may speak for themselves, they are heard through culturally conditioned ears.

Many managers, however, don't take to the idea that one of their important duties is to manage their organizational cultures. Cultures are too soft, foggy, unclear. Managers want more substantive realities to work with. Maybe that's why they have so often ignored their cultures, leaving them to shape and reshape themselves—often to the managers' detriment.

Can anything more relevant to management be said about the nature of organizational cultures? A good deal.

● We know that company founders have a very great impact on the cultures of their organizations, an impact that

---

* "Air-Ways," *Financial Times*, London, England, December 5, 1984, p. 16.

often lasts for generations. So #1 issues are relevant to organizational culture.

- The explicit and implicit messages recurrently transmitted by an organization's leaders become a major force in shaping the organization's culture. The stories that are passed on from generation to generation help to carry a company's culture along, just as they do in all other kinds of cultures.
- Organizational cultures aren't shaped in a day. They take a long time to form.
- Problems arise when an organization's culture differs sharply from that of the larger society around it, because members of the organization must also remain members of their larger societies. Great gaps between the two quickly generate anger, suspicion, and rejection.
- Organizational cultures are not necessarily internally rational and coherent. Subcultures, even countercultures, form and re-form within larger parent cultures, causing tensions that can result in revolution and collapse or in innovation and creation.
- We know that outside enemies are powerful shapers of our cultures. The fact that there are bad guys out there helps us to know that we are the good guys.
- And we know that while it's hard to confine and define a culture, it's even more difficult to change one.

Since the concept of organizational culture has been so faddish in the last three or four years, the whole idea may be over the hill by the time this book goes to press. But it shouldn't be. The concept of culture is important and useful for managers. It provides a handle for thinking, on a company-wide scale, about both the human and the control sides of the enterprise. Until now, in America at least, we have approached the human issues of our companies mostly in a very micro way, thinking always about individuals and small groups, envisioning the organization as either a pyramid of individuals (in the old days) or a pyramid of small groups piled up on one another (in recent years). The concept of culture opens up a third way of thinking about the human side of the enterprise—a total way. It gives the manager a means of thinking about and working with the human aspects of the whole organization, of viewing the organization as a human community, like a tribe or an extended family. And when one starts thinking that way, many powerful managerial possibilities begin to emerge.

The people who know more about cultures than anyone else are the anthropologists. But like the *Enterprise* crew in *Star Trek*, they discover and observe cultures but try very hard not to interfere with them. Managers are different. They interfere with cultures all the time, actively trying to reshape and remodel old ones and to invent new ones. That's a hard job, in part because cultures are so difficult to get hold of, in part because the pieces are so complexly interconnected that if you change one component of a culture, you may get unimagined effects in other components.

Before we get on with questions of culture building, at least two caveats are in order: First, you don't manage organizational culture by setting up a new Director of Culture Management. It's too big, too pervasive a job for that. Throwing a title at it won't build a culture.

Second, the moment we adopt a let's-try-to-manage-the-company-culture posture, huge ethical questions immediately arise. When we say we want to manage our company's culture, isn't that about equivalent to saying we want to brainwash our people into believing and feeling as we do?

Yes, indeed! Companies that try to manage cultures usually do so to gain loyalty, to get people to become believers, and to win support for company causes. But that's not unusual. Governments have long known how important supportive public opinion can be to successful governing, and they usually know a lot about how to shape it. Cultural management in an organization also aims at shaping the passions, loyalties, and identifications of all the organization's members. So it is not surprising that serious questions of ethics, justice, and autonomy always ride along in the same compartment.

Given those front-end cautions, we can go on to more specific ideas about developing and managing cultures. Here is a summary set of relevant points:

- Culture building, we said earlier, is a long, ongoing process. And cultures are not shaped by company creeds cast on bronze plaques. They are shaped by #1 beliefs, communicated again and again, day in and day out, through #3 acts.

- To manage culture means to say and do things every day that begin to make people feel that they are all members of the same tribe, to create "sameness."

    Organizations can create sameness in all sorts of ways, including some scary ones. One common method is to require sameness in behavior. By standardizing and restricting what people actively do, we can hope that underlying feelings and faiths will fall into place. The trouble with that method is that when we take the pressure off, much of the sameness immediately disappears. The sameness doesn't always penetrate deeply into the blood.

    Nevertheless, many organizations use methods like those for building cultures. Armies put people into uniforms, shave their heads, and march them in unison to inculcate the army culture. But uniforms are not just worn by the military. School kids in many parts of the world also wear them. Many Japanese companies put their employees in uniform. In America, we impose explicit or implicit dress codes too, including three-piece suits and striped ties. And the "uniforms" of boys have been kept quite different from the uniforms of girls in most of the world's cultures.

- Another way to build cultural sameness in belief and thought is to set up a series of filters that screen out differences, so that those who have passed through all the filters are quite alike. A colleague of mine once enraged a group of large-company vice presidents by asserting that by the time a manager becomes a VP, he has passed through so many filters that he is like a light bulb. No one cares much about which particular VP you get, because you're sure that almost any one of them will work about as well as any other. The danger in that filtering process is that it may work too well, especially at the top of the organization. Diversity of ideas can gradually disappear. But we certainly apply that filtering mechanism in most of our organizations. We select and promote "good" exponents of the culture's beliefs and values.

  While such efforts really do help build cultures, the use of external pressures for that purpose can, as we all know, easily backfire. The cultures we build in that way can become countercultures, hostile to the organization, because the organization has tried too hard to squeeze its members into restrictively uniform behavior.

- Long-term culture management requires much more than dress codes, standardized behaviors, and the promotion of good citizens. It requires the *management of meanings*—developing a special system of meanings that members of the organization share. That's not a new idea. Managers have always consciously tried to manage meaning *outside* their organization, by trying to influence their customers' valuation of their products and by trying to develop a public image of their organization as a legitimate and worthy citizen. The management of internal meanings is just as important.

● Some of what any organizational culture is all about is defined by an organization's relationship with other organizations. Managing organizational culture includes the important task of managing the meanings of other organizations around us. Who are our friends? Who are our enemies? Salient, threatening enemies are great catalysts for creativity, urgency, and togetherness. If the invasion of such an enemy is imminent, even the most phlegmatic among us will find the will and the energy to take up arms. Given such an enemy, second lieutenants will have a much easier time in controlling and motivating their troops.

But enemies have to be worthy and salient, and it is not always easy to find such enemies. The leaders of Apple Computer can stir up the spirits of their people by conjuring up visions of the hot breath of the big blue IBM monster. But IBM's leaders would have trouble reversing the process. Apples, for IBM, are small potatoes. For Westerners, at least, enemies have to be big and strong if they are to give common meaning to our people, to function as culture builders. Preferably they should be bigger and stronger than we are. We need Goliaths as enemies, not Davids.

And just suppose we win. The foe is vanquished! What then? Enemies are useful for managerial culture building, but their usefulness usually extends only over the short term.

● The stories, myths, and legends, whether true or false, that get passed along to newcomers help define and transmit the organization's culture. Stories like these send symbolic signals:

> One Saturday the CEO got a hacksaw and cut off the lock on the supply room door. He wanted people to feel free to get their supplies when they needed them.

> In the old days, the founder set up a clinic in an old school bus out in the desert. For a nickel a day he provided full medical care to the poor families stuck out there in the heat. And he did it even though the American Medical Association fought him every step of the way.
>
> "Nuts!" said our general when the Germans demanded his surrender.
>
> When the boss caught old Joe Smith snitching paper clips, he fired Joe on the spot, even though Joe had 20 years of service.

- Physical design helps shape culture. Open offices? Sixty-story steel and glass headquarters? Contemporary furniture? Private executive dining rooms? All of those carry meanings about what the culture is like. So do the colors of the drapes, the paintings on the walls, and every other physical detail.

- Rituals and other symbolic acts are also important carriers of culture. Morning meetings, annual picnics, award ceremonies—all play a part. Informal rituals and routines are probably even more important. Does everyone say "Good morning" to everyone else every day? Do we lunch together every Thursday? Do we have a drink together after work on Friday? How about company flags?

> In one company the CEO and other senior officers hand-built the table in their conference room. They treat the table as a kind of shrine.
>
> The research director of a large lab has breakfast each day with a different first-line supervisor.
>
> Whenever our building is visited by someone from overseas, we run up the flag of his country.
>
> The first Tuesday of each month is the department head's open office day. Coffee and cookies are served.

And so on, with symbolic rituals that characterize our people, our culture—both our commonality and our uniqueness.

- And let's not forget the special vocabularies of organizations. Almost all organizations develop unique meanings for words. I was puzzled for a long time by the use of a common word in an uncommon way at a company I consulted with. The word was *stimulate*. Someone would say, "Harry got stimulated last week." I finally learned that in that organization "stimulate" meant "fire." To stimulate people was to fire them—that is, to stimulate them to go somewhere else. Does that say anything about the culture? I doubt that people from that organization ever die. They probably "depart."

From all of these—the stories told to newcomers, the decor in the cafeteria, the size of the CEO's office—the people of an organization evolve a shared dictionary of the organization's meanings. Those meanings are important in the same way that a code book is important. They tell the receiver what each small signal *really* means, and they also tell the receiver that he is an insider, a member of the tribe.

Managing a culture thus becomes a combination of #1 ideas with the #3 implementing process, requiring a continuing alertness by managers to make sure that they are creating the meanings they want to create. Every act, every memo, carries those second-order signals with it. It's a hard but not impossible task, so long as managers know what they're trying to build. All of this is simply to say that the single most powerful *local* force for shaping an organization's culture is its leadership. The most powerful *general* force is the larger societal culture in which the organization is embedded. The messages, intended and unintended, sent out by an organization's leaders define the broad direction in which that organization's culture will evolve.

Changing old cultures: Can managers move mountains?

If it's an old culture, new messages from new leaders may not have much impact, at least for a long time. The first generation of leaders, the founders, are the critically important figures because they write on a blank slate. They don't have to remodel old cultures. Their influence is therefore more quickly and intensely felt. From the beginning, they set the rules and the styles of the organization. They select the people, specify the physical setup, work out reward systems, and all the rest. It's not surprising, therefore, that when we try to name those who are most effective in building strong organizational cultures, we almost always name founders—from the Founding Fathers of the United States to the founders of IBM or Standard Oil.

Later generations of leaders have a tougher problem on their hands. They must manage existing cultures, trying either to maintain or change them. Usually they can effect only incremental changes, and many of them don't do that, because they are selected to continue the old culture, not to replace it.

But if we want to reshape an old culture significantly, we can add at least three items to our list of culture shapers:

● Crises—wars, revolutions, recessions—are great looseners of old cultures. They make it far easier for leaders to effect radical changes, even in stolid, traditional cultures. We have all seen that happen in great national crises— the American or the French or the Russian revolutions— but it also happens in organizations. Old roles and boundaries give way in crises.

During World War II, for example, women moved into jobs previously reserved to men. Junior officers could be promoted over their seniors. (Lieutenant Colonel Eisenhower was kicked up to general overnight.)

Ideas for new ways to do old jobs were welcomed rather than ignored. Inventiveness flourished in technology and education as well as in military tactics. While we dropped back partway after the war, some of the changes (for example, the emergence of new work roles for women) stuck and even started chains of further changes both in our national culture and in the cultures of industrial organizations. Is the Chrysler turnaround under Lee Iacocca a fair example of an old culture changing in a crisis? Perhaps Iacocca could have done it even if Chrysler had not been on the verge of bankruptcy, but the crisis surely enabled faster change.

Crises, moreover, are relative matters. Their meanings can often be managed and they often are. When, for instance, does a crisis become a crisis? Would the Cuban missile crisis necessarily have been defined as a crisis if someone else had been in the White House? Or would it have been a "serious problem"? Would a 10 percent drop in quarterly revenues constitute a "crisis" in your company? If so, why? If not, why not? Some of the answer has to lie in the meanings given to events by managers. The meanings of organizational events, like the meanings of personal events, are always partially manageable.

● Even without the dramatic help of wars or recessions, a new leader, by sheer force of personal style, will occasionally succeed in generating a radical new organizational culture. We don't see such turnarounds very often, but occasionally they show up. Robert Hutchins turned the University of Chicago's culture around a few decades ago. Ren McPherson seemed to have done it at Dana Corporation. And most readers can probably point to a few executives who, even without the help of crises, have been able to build a completely new culture where an old one used to be.

● A third device for changing an old culture is so obvious
that we might easily miss it. Change the people. Cultures
are carried in people. One way to change a culture is to
get rid of the old people and replace them with new
ones.

That's often done, of course, and it can be a cruel
and painful process. Sometimes it doesn't work, usually
because the surgery isn't radical enough. When we
change just a few people at a time, the old culture may
change the newcomers more than they change the culture. Or if we just change the top team, we may succeed
only in setting up an adversarial battle between the top
and the rest of the organization. In such wars, organizations often defeat their leaders.

Culture building: A #1–#3 combination

Whether they are founders or later generations of leaders, just what is it that people do to rebuild and reshape
organizational cultures? Much of what they do can be
wrapped up in one sentence: They define and communicate
a clear organizational mission.

That seems simple enough. All it takes is knowing the
way (that's the #1 part) and then pointing that way out so
clearly and so often that everyone can see it, while at the
same time convincing everyone that it's the right way to go
(that's the #3 part of the parlay). The ability to define a clear
mission, communicate it, and persuade others to join up
constitutes one definition of leadership—not the nitty-gritty
administrative kind of leadership but what one political sci-
entist called "transformational" leadership, the kind of visionary leadership that opens up new worlds.

Mission making is a #1 pathfinding job calling for imagination and determination. It is usually the harder part of the
parlay, especially for action-oriented executives. It requires

much more inward than outward action. It requires pause, introspection, self-analysis, and a long-range and wide-angle view of one's world.

Culture building is its #3 partner, a job calling for communication, persuasion, and personal demonstration. That's where the rituals come in. Heroes, "good" enemies, flags, war dances, and schmaltz can all play their parts in the implementing part of the act. In America, we go for trumpets and pep talks, laurel wreaths, and management-by-wandering-around as preferred tools for putting a particular organizational culture into place. In other societies, different and less flamboyant methods may be in order. In Italy, social class and family may play a large part; in Australia, it can be "mateship" among men (or more properly, "miteship"); in Japan, calisthenics and Shinto rituals; and the French just eat together.

Some individuals are great at that emotional #3 part of culture building. They find it easy, even pleasant, to beat the drums and lead the dances. They have a sense of drama. They carry an aura of excitement and urgency with them wherever they go. Such emotional injections represent a side of the managing process that has been sorely neglected by the cool "professional" executives of recent history. Only sales departments seem to have been able to keep that flavor alive.

We've come back in recent years toward a greater appreciation of the importance of that unsophisticated, emotional, human side of getting things done in organizations— and a greater appreciation of those who have the skills to do it.

But to effect cultural change, or to maintain the vitality of existing cultures, those #3 techniques of communication and influence need a solid #1 base. They need a clear, simple, honest vision of where the organization wants to go and what the rules are for getting there. Without those, any form of hype is just hype.

Socialization: The cultural production line

We haven't used the word *socialization* much until now. It's an important idea. Socialization is the major mechanism by which a culture is transmitted from generation to generation and from person to person. Socialization, the whole array of influences exerted by members of a community on one another, is the production line of culture. The raw materials go in at one end and the fully acculturated member comes out at the other. First, parents "teach" their children the rules and standards; then the peer group takes over; then school, church, and company pick up the task. But this kind of teaching isn't like classroom teaching. Socialization is a continuous, emotional sandpapering process designed to teach the rules of the game through the application of a multitude of everyday rewards, punishments, and examples. The punishments may range from quietly communicated expectations, to cold impatience, to the silent treatment, to withdrawal of resources, to physical attack, to isolation and dismissal from the group. The positive rewards may range from pats on the head, to monetary rewards, to ritual initiations into full tribal membership—often replete with a formal oath promising unswerving adherence to the rules.

Certain classes of managers typically know a great deal about how to use socialization techniques to build cultures. For expert assistance, try the commanding officer of a Marine Corps boot camp, or the mother superior of the nearest convent, or the high school football coach. They know many ways to speed up and focus the socialization process.

One way is total immersion. You don't go home to dinner and TV after an eight-hour shift at the convent. It's 24 hours every day. Add uniforms to increase feelings of—sure enough—uniformity; and add regularly repeated activities that require public participation, from parades to prayers. Action, after all, is a foot in the door to attitude change.

The manager, however, despite his power to hire and fire, is not usually the most important cultural socializer in an organization. The peer group can almost always do a faster and better job.

Peer groups can do the job better for a couple of obvious reasons: They are usually physically closer to the new member for more of the time. Physical proximity increases the power of social rewards and punishments enormously. And groups are plural. Several people together can be more powerful socializers than a single person. When those other people are right there, right now, across the table, staring at you and waiting for your answer, that's pressure. When a memo or a videotape comes down from the CEO, that may help, but that's not hand-to-hand combat. That's just the sound of distant artillery fire.

If the reader has sensed a somewhat manipulative, Machiavellian quality in the last few paragraphs, it was intentional. The intent was to highlight the enormously complex ethical questions that must accompany the power to socialize. That power is real, whether one labels it education or brainwashing. Some people, if they control physical or psychological resources, can effectively shape the beliefs, values, and behaviors of other people in almost any direction. When managers decide to "manage" their company's cultures, they are taking on a heavy moral responsibility as well as a heavy workload.

One more major warning about changing old organizational cultures: Don't try to build an organizational culture that is even more different from the larger surrounding culture than the old one already in place.

Most socializing has already been done by society at large before people ever get to the organization. Managers had better assess the whole triangle—the distances between the culture they want to build and both the old organizational culture and the larger culture that already surrounds the organization. The greater the distances of the new from the old and from the surround, the more difficult and dangerous the job will be. The job will be more difficult because you will have to get both veterans and new recruits to give up their old ways before they can take on your new ones and because if the old culture gets a lot of support from the outside culture, it will be even more resistant to change. The job will be more dangerous because larger cultures often stomp on smaller subcultures that insist on playing by their own rules. Deviant new religions are banned; deviant companies are regulated, or sued, or picketed, or boycotted. And the adverse reaction is even greater when the newcomer tries to squeeze out the respectable old-timers.

Churches and armies have faced analogous problems. They typically try to bridge the gap between their cultures and the cultures of the surrounding societies by costly but powerful techniques of isolating and totally immersing their recruits. The modern, and much weaker, organizational equivalents are retreats and training programs.

The issue of distance between cultures triggers related questions: What about mergers with, or takeovers of, organizations that already have other cultures in place? What about overseas subsidiaries, units that are part of *our* company but part of *their* culture?

I once attended a management meeting of a French company that had recently acquired several other small French companies. Even more recently it had acquired a small German company. Everybody was at the meeting. At dinner on the first night, the CEO took me aside and said, "See that group at that table over there? The ones with the neckties on? Those are the Germans. The real reason for this meeting is to try to make them part of this company. We don't wear neckties!" After dinner, the CEO led group singing and storytelling. He got the German manager to tell a story and then to lead the French in a German drinking song. The evening went on until morning. By the next day, most of the German executives had almost become members of the company culture.

The answers remain the same. But the greater the gap between the cultures, the greater is the amount of energy, emotion, and other resources that will be required to build a moderately common company culture.

It costs a lot less, and it is a lot easier, either to marry organizations with already similar cultures or to build organizational cultures that are fundamentally consonant with their surrounding cultural environments, even though they have a few unique attributes of their own.

Bell Telephone Laboratories, before the breakup of AT&T, provided an excellent example of an organization that profited enormously by staying close to its relevant wider culture. For many decades, Bell Labs has been, in the eyes of almost all observers, the preeminent industrial research laboratory in the world. It has spawned a number of Nobel prizewinners as well as a host of major advances in basic and applied science and technology. One reason may be that the gap between the BTL culture and the then *relevant* surrounding culture was always kept very small. Bell Labs recruits were selected from a set that had already been presocialized into a common system of beliefs and values— graduate students from university departments of engineering and science. By the time young Bell Labs technical recruits joined the organization, they had typically already been socialized into the strong, clear culture of the world of science and technology. During their university education they had been taught to value objectivity, empiricism, and intellectual integrity. Just as the Japanese company carries on the underlying values of Japanese culture, BTL simply carried on the existing values of technological culture, from the university on into its labs. BTL recruited from that subgroup of American kids who had been ham radio operators and math whizzes. In their early years in high school or even earlier, many of those kids had been rather isolated and often denigrated members of minority subcultures. They were the science nuts, the nerds, the "brains." But for such nerds and brains, working at BTL was like entry into heaven. The things that they already valued were the same things that the company valued: curiosity, competence, dedication, creativity. Promotion was much more a matter of technical than of managerial skill. Indeed, managerial skill was, for a long time, considered insignificant, to be left to such second-class citizens as accountants and administrators.

So while those shared values had been initially inculcated earlier and elsewhere, they were effectively utilized and fostered by BTL through its selection processes and its management practice.

BTL was, and is, a wonderful national and world resource. The fact that it chose to build on its technological culture, to create a place where a technologist could really feel at home, was itself a pathfinding act. But, it is important to note, a changing world has come to demand of BTL things that its kind of culture cannot easily give—things like sensitivity to the marketplace and a competitive, killer instinct. The BTL culture of the 70s and early 80s was not set up to design Mickey Mouse telephones.

Strong purposive cultures, even those consonant with their surrounds, can be entrapped by changes in their economic and political conditions and driven from their isolated mountaintops. But the other extreme has its problems too. Highly reactive organizations, responsive to every little change in the environmental breeze, can spend so much time and energy twisting and dodging that they fail to distinguish the important from the unimportant.

It's worth noting that such companies as BTL have a lot in common with many Japanese organizations, at least in the relationship between the company culture and the larger outside culture. Large Japanese companies draw their recruits from an intensely presocialized population. Long before young Japanese enter the company, they are taught attitudes of conformity and self-subordination. Those attitudes fit nicely into later organizational life. Recruits already socialized into obedience, respect for authority, and a readiness to give a deep commitment to the company make the Japanese manager's job fairly easy compared to what American managers often face.

Large Japanese companies also encourage wide participation in planning and decision making at all levels, to a degree that we sometimes find astonishing. But that's possible because their strong cultures almost guarantee that their well-socialized people will make decisions within the acceptable bounds that have already been predefined by earlier socialization processes.

So building any kind of organizational culture, either a brand-new one or a replacement, takes some doing. And building a pathfinding organizational culture takes even more doing. The next chapter is about the particular problems and characteristics of that special class of cultures, pathfinding organizational cultures.

BUILDING PATHFINDING CULTURES:
Toward Plural and Parallel Pathfinding

All managers, whether they intend it or not, are culture builders. Pathfinding managers typically build stronger cultures faster than nonpathfinding managers. But pathfinding managers do not always build pathfinding cultures. Pathfinding managers tend to want to run the show. They hold the pathfinding role mostly to themselves. They want others to be followers, not leaders; planners and implementers, not more pathfinders. So they often build other kinds of organizational cultures, but not pathfinding cultures.

Until now this book has not discussed different kinds of organizational cultures, but obviously there are many. Some are passive, obedient, disciplined. People do what they're told and follow the rules. Some are ebullient, loud, raucous. People shout at each other, play practical jokes, slam doors in anger. Some are dedicated and hardworking. People are committed to the work and to the company's cause. Some, the pathfinding cultures, are creative, imaginative, a little anarchistic. People go off in their own directions and fight for their own causes. Organizational cultures can be any combination of the above, and a lot more. Organizational cultures are as divergent as fingerprints. No two are alike.

But some organizational cultures have much more of a pathfinding flavor than others. And this chapter is about the conditions most likely to produce such cultures.

Pathfinding leaders and pathfinding cultures: Does A cause B?

Organizational life, like the rest of life, is full of paradoxes. Among them is the fact that pathfinding leaders often produce nonpathfinding organizations. Imaginative leaders often attract unimaginative followers, and powerful leaders often generate powerless subordinates. When Papa knows all the answers and has all the ideas, the kids may learn only to carry out his commands.

It's not very hard to find examples of that strong leader/ dependent follower phenomenon. Prime Minister Lee Kuan Yew of Singapore may be one of this century's most impressive pathfinders, having built that city-state from nothing to a successful, highly educated, high-income society in a matter of about 20 years. But as of this writing, he has himself expressed concern about his nation's excessive dependency on him and about its shortage of vigorous creativity. The length of his own shadow has surely been one of the major reasons that not very many other flowers have bloomed. Lee has been so successful that most of his people look more to him for answers than to themselves.

Many companies have followed a similar path. The brilliant leadership of Edwin Land at Polaroid did not seem to generate large amounts of pathfinding among people down the line. Nor did the dominance of Harold Geneen at ITT. And the reader can surely identify other cases, closer to home, of pathfinding leadership that failed to reseed itself.

Most of the time, dominance by powerful, visionary leaders is neither malevolent nor intentional. Very creative, very independent, very stubborn people are not usually easy to live with, especially in organizations. And when such people add the ownership of economic resources to the resources of their own intellects, they usually run the show. They often try to run it even when it gets to be a big show; and they are apt to fail. Some of those brilliant, charismatic leaders, however, manage to run even very big shows very well indeed—for as long as they live.

So caveat 1: The fact that pathfinding leaders are in place at the top does *not* mean that a pathfinding organizational culture will surely be found down below. That doesn't mean that such a culture *won't* ever be found down the line, but pathfinding leaders very often produce dependent, unimaginative offspring who don't look at all like their parents.

Probably the single leadership act that is most likely to help generate a pathfinding culture is a particular kind of mission emanating from the top—a mission that focuses much more on *people* than on products or services. A pathfinding culture—one in which a climate of creativity and determination pervades the whole organization—certainly needs pathfinding leadership, but it needs leadership committed to building just that kind of pathfinding culture. Not all organizational missions, not all pathfinding leaders, aim at that.

The possibilities for #1 missions are divergent and endless; and most of those missions will not contribute to pathfinding cultures. Are we trying to become the trimmest and tautest ship in the fleet—scrubbed down, efficient, disciplined? Are we trying to become the world's biggest producer of jet widgets? Are we trying to become the fastest gun in the West, faster than any other to the market with new styles, new colors, new products? Are we dedicated first to profit? to our stockholders? Or are we dedicated to bringing the blessings of electronic horseshoes to all humanity?

All those are missions for organizations, and any of them may be deeply believed and stubbornly pursued by the organization's leaders and followers. But none of them is, by itself, likely to produce a pervasively pathfinding culture of innovativeness and entrepreneurship.

Parallel and plural pathfinding cultures

One major target needed to build pathfinding cultures is simply the target of wanting to build pathfinding cultures—putting that very high on the priority list, believing in it, preaching it, working on it, and communicating to everyone the value that pathfinding is everybody's job. The implicit model for a pathfinding culture is *not* the three-tiered model of specialized pathfinders at the top, specialized problem solvers in the middle, and specialized implementers at the bottom. What is required is a *parallel* and *plural* rather than a *serial* and *singular* vision of the desired organization. It is a vibrant vision, one that essentially encourages everybody to get into the whole managing process—to create, to solve problems, to implement.

That parallel, plural model departs rather radically from

more usual alternative views of what a good organization should look like. Most of us have grown up debating the costs and benefits of two other views: A good organization is either an orderly, hierarchical, specialized, and authoritarian #2 type—out of the military tradition; or it is a humanistic, participative #3 type—democratic, cooperative, and team oriented. For many reasons, most of our present-day organizations were in fact built first on #2 authoritarian and hierarchical foundations. Later, we did a partial remodeling job to add on some #3 participative components.

While the prominent characteristics of a *pathfinding* culture have more in common with the participative #3 models than with the authoritarian #2 models, such cultures are quite different from either of the other two.

- Pathfinding organizations are more like "organized anarchies" than like either formal bureaucracies or group-based participative systems. By rational standards, that is, pathfinding organizational cultures look chaotic, impulsive, subjective, and hectic. By participative #3 standards, they may look individualistically aggressive, competitive, and insensitive. Pathfinding organizations will look disorganized to some observers and overly aggressive to others because they focus on inspiration, experimentation, and pushing things through. They do not give first priority to either formal protocol or warm interpersonal relationships. Indeed, they typically don't worry much about such physical amenities as carpeted offices either. They are not primarily concerned with either standardized processes and practices or with mutual support and security—though both must ultimately be incorporated into the service of getting things done.

- Pathfinding cultures often show high rates of internal piracy. Filching and smuggling of people, and sometimes materials, from one another can be quite commonplace.

They may be seen as acceptable, just so long as it is clear that those acts are aimed at getting the work done.

- Unlike, say, stereotypical Japanese-style management, pathfinding cultures support deviant behavior by individuals and by groups, encouraging both to push their own ideas and to resist pressures to conform.

- Not surprisingly, pathfinding cultures often give more points to youthful vigor, imagination, and enthusiasm than to the stability and wisdom of the sage elders.

- If you walk in on a pathfinding culture, you may see a lot of goofing off, fooling around—and on company time! High emotional intensity, minimal structure, and more spontaneous groups all lead quite naturally toward what may look like wasteful foolishness, especially to the eyes of more traditional folk. Sometimes it really is foolishness, but such temporary relaxations of the normal rules serve more positive purposes. Who of us cannot recall occasions (especially when we were young) when we kicked over the traces, acting childishly silly and playful? But those were often also occasions associated with prior periods of intensely creative and imaginative search and exploration. For some of us, growing up has meant giving up such playful periods altogether; but people close to research settings will surely recognize that such episodes of childlike foolishness are highly functional. They release tensions, and more important, they eliminate, albeit temporarily, inhibitions to creative thought.

- Once again, however, a caution. While pathfinding organizations almost always exhibit rewarding periods of foolishness, it doesn't necessarily work the other way around. The context is critical. Adding more parties, games, and funny hats might help disinhibit an organization and *might* thereby help move it toward more pathfinding; but plugged into a maximum security organization, such devices may produce more bad hangovers than great ideas.

- Pathfinding approaches share an important value with the #3 participative models. They both hold to Theory Y assumptions about people. That is, they assume that people fundamentally like to work and also possess a natural capacity for ingenuity and creativity. Like the participative models, the pathfinding models encourage open, informal, and frequent communication. But participative organizations tend to subordinate individuals to groups and try to reduce individual tensions and anxiety. Pathfinding-type organizations, however, pay relatively more attention to innovative urgency than to emotional well-being, and to the creativity of group members than to mutual trust and understanding.

- The people most valued in pathfinding organizations are likely to be innovative champions, risk takers, entrepreneurs. Such people are not always courteous, kind, and cooperative. They may be abrasive pains-in-the-neck. So in pathfinding organizations, the rest of us may wonder about the justice of it all.

- Pathfinding cultures typically exercise their controls less frequently than do #2 or #3 types of organizations, allowing their people longer time spans of discretion and more chances to try things out before being called to account.

   In contrast, #2-type organizations tend to control frequently. They try to get the flexibility they need by making sure that they received quick feedback about everything that is going on in the organization. The more participative #3-type organizations also tend to exercise frequent control, but it is more informal peer control.

- In their *In Search of Excellence*,[1] Peters and Waterman used the salient phrase "simultaneous tight-loose" properties to describe one aspect of their excellent organizations. That phrase catches very well the flavor of those somewhat loose, anarchistic pathfinding cultures, which are at the same time firm and tight about a few inviolable organizational commandments; commandments like "Thou shalt not let a substandard product out of the plant" or "Thou shalt not ever fudge any data." In pathfinding organizations, incidentally, such commandments seldom intrude on personal lifestyles. Pathfinding organizations don't have commandments about haircuts or dress codes, and they need not, though some do, have commandments about how people treat one another.

- Implicitly, but pervasively, pathfinding cultures place a high value on the intrinsic importance and enjoyment of the work itself, as in Andrew Carnegie's only known quotable line: "My heart is in the work!" They want and expect work to be central and to be fun.

- While many pathfinding cultures were started by their founders a good while back, they are almost always actively *future* oriented. They think and talk about what we will or might do next, and about where to go from here. It is not possible to maintain a pathfinding culture in an organization that chooses a static posture. If, for example, a unit is defined by its leaders to be a cash cow (an unfortunate but descriptive phrase) to be milked of its existing capacities, then it cannot also be a future-oriented, experimental pathfinding organization. Notice that we are back to the management of meaning here. If we define the unit as a cash cow, or a dog, we sharply increase the likelihood that its members will behave accordingly.

- It will come as no surprise that members of pathfinding-flavored cultures don't worry very much about staying within channels or about bypassing levels of command. People go where they feel they need to go, and they talk to whom they need to talk. Protocol almost becomes a dirty word.

In this respect, pathfinding styles will seem more familiar to some professions than to others. Academics and scientists will easily understand that aspect of path-finding styles. The norms of the cultures of academia and science operate in much the same way. It is knowledge and competence rather than rank that count. The focus is less on one's status, more on one's work. Young scientists can feel fairly free to argue matters of science with their seniors. Assistant professors can talk back to full professors—on matters of research. Pathfinding organizations usually extend those norms to a wider range of task-relevant matters, to issues of design, markets, procedures, services. In pathfinding cultures, seniors seldom give orders to subordinates and frequently seek their counsel.

Some other professions, however, find the bypassing of lines of authority abhorrent and dangerous. Diplomats don't usually like the idea, and many older senior executives are horrified by such breaches of organizational discipline.

● Pathfinding organizations worry much more about controlling outcomes than about controlling processes. The focus is more on getting it done, less on the right way to do it; more on urgent effort, less on arbitrary deadlines. There are no 50-second work cycles here, no formal daily evaluations of progress. Imaginative turned-on people make their own assessments of themselves and of those around them. And they generally use very tough standards.

● Notice that in this regard pathfinding-type organizations are not altogether different from the upper levels of many other organizations. Senior executives don't undergo daily inspections, nor are they given detailed procedural programs to follow, nor do they punch in and out. Pathfinding organizations simply extend that expectation of self-control and self-starting throughout the company.

- So far, we have only hinted at another important issue. What about the relationship between pathfinding cultures and youth? It is the young who seem always to invigorate the world, to challenge sacred cows, and to wave proudly, though perhaps naively, the banner of idealism. If so, then building a more pathfinding organization ought to include not only some continuous input of young, fresh people but also some active exploitation of those attributes. Pathfinding organizations usually do that. They follow the advice that St. Benedict gave (in A.D. 529) about the right way to run an abbey. When something really important came up, St. Benedict urged the abbot to call *everybody* together and to hear their advice. "Now the reason why we have said that all should be called to council," St. Benedict wrote, "is that God often reveals what is better to the younger . . ." But "when the work to be done in the interests of the monastery is of lesser importance, let [the abbot] use the advice of the seniors only."[2]

   Reluctantly, at my age, I must agree that youth, dreams, and a drive to improve the world still tend to hang together, at least in our Western cultures. It's the innocent young who are likely to be the first to notice that the emperor has no clothes. And they will announce that fact too, in loud, clear voices. It's the innocent young who don't know that it can't be done, who strut their arrogant self-assurance, driving us cynical veterans to despair. But it's also the young who, most of the time, start the new fires. The Don Quixotes of the real world are almost always young.

   Even the young grow old, however. Over time their organizations can get to them. They are socialized. They are coopted by the system. They begin to accept the unacceptable and to tolerate the intolerable.

Bringing young people into organizations is therefore a mechanism for incremental change. Even while they are challenging the organization, the organization is sandpapering them into conformity. With luck, both will change a little.

But there's no free lunch here either. Not all young people are either imaginative or idealistic. It's too easy to find plenty who have already become passive and pliable. So the recruitment of young people cannot in itself be taken as evidence of a search for a pathfinding culture.

The role of small groups in pathfinding organizations

Small groups have become such an important structural unit in all modern approaches to organizational design that they deserve a special discussion here. For while small groups play an important role in pathfinding organizations, it is a role quite different from the one they play in either classical #2 or participative #3 designs. In order to get a better fix on the contributory role that small groups can play in moving an organization toward a more pathfinding culture, it's important first to look back a little at the emergence of the small group as a key unit in organizational thought.

For managers in traditional #2 command-and-control-type organizations, the word *group* usually meant trouble. Particularly in the 1920s and 30s, when jobs were designed for individuals and individual incentives prevailed, group interaction was often actively discouraged by managers. It interfered with work, and it might mean that workers would talk union.

Groups always formed anyway, informally. They were tougher to kill off than cockroaches. Often those informal lunchtime or after-work groups found their common mission in fighting the system—making sure that the time study man didn't set the times too fast, initiating new people so that they wouldn't become rate-busters, developing alarm systems to warn when supervisors were approaching. For managers who wanted fast, steady, uncomplaining work, using prespecified methods, such groups were anathema. They were the seedbeds of discontent and resistance.

By the late 1950s, however, as more participative models gained a foothold, much more positive meanings began to be attributed to small groups. From the shop floor on up, appreciation of the potential productive power of small groups increased. Stimulated by such people as Kurt Lewin at MIT and Fritz Roethlisberger at Harvard, interest in small work groups surged forward. Roethlisberger, for example, with singular insight describes how groups and social relationships had looked to him at Western Electric's Hawthorne Works way back in the 1920s:

Whenever and wherever it was possible, [employees] generated [these informal groups] like crazy. In many cases they found them so satisfying that they often did all sorts of nonlogical things (that is, things that went counter to their economic interests) in order to belong to the small, warm, and cozy groups which these relations generated. . . .

The two kinds of relations were in sharp contrast. Among members of hierarchical relations, there were few interactions, few close friendships, and seldom any small, warm, cozy groups. There was sometimes "respect," but quite often distrust, apprehension, and suspicion.

It was an unconscious battle between the logic of management and the sentiments of workers.[3]*

---

* From F. J. Roethlisberger, *The Elusive Phenomena: An Autobiographical Account of My Work in the Field of Organizational Behavior at the Harvard Business School,* edited by George F. F. Lombard. Boston: Division of Research, Harvard Business School, 1977, pp. 165–66.

In the next few decades, social scientists and managers alike came to understand the potential positive power of those informal groups. They began to integrate groups into the organization instead of trying to stamp them out. As the participative models evolved, small work groups began to be defined as friends of the organization, not as its enemies. They became major tools of organizational development. Groups could serve emotional ends by building loyalty and commitment. They could serve disciplinary and socializing ends by teaching new people the ropes and by pressing conformity to group (and company) norms. They could serve motivational ends by providing feelings of purposiveness and loyalty.

In that same period, the concept of leadership was being reshaped. It was seen less and less as a matter of personal charisma and more and more as a set of functions for getting effective commitment from group members. Good leaders were people who made sure that everyone was heard, that personal hostilities got ironed out, that agreement was achieved. *Group process* became a key idea. If we can learn to communicate with one another in a valid and trusting way, then we can work more effectively on any substantive problem. And that was not at all a silly idea!

The earlier notions, that groups were threats to managerial authority, gave way to a focus on small groups as a key structural unit in organizational design, a mediating bridge between the whole organization and each individual member. Team building came to the fore, enlarging and enriching jobs and opening up more self-control by groups over their special areas of work.

In some northern European nations those groupy, participative approaches have long since been institutionalized into law, sometimes in ways that look strange to us. Norway, for example, requires supervisors, by law, to make their people's jobs as participative and enriching as possible. In Japan small groups also serve as a powerful mechanism for controlling the organization's behavior. So pervasively are the Japanese identified with groups that Westerners joke about never encountering just one Japanese at a time.

In the United States we have quietly moved very far toward organizations in which small groups—variously called task forces, project teams, or committees—play an incontrovertibly important role. In a recent discussion I had with several very senior managers, for instance, each of them commented that that was one big way in which management practice had changed since their early years—more small groups now, more giving and taking of counsel and advice, more persuasion, less top-down command.

Yet we, in America, still feel negative about small groups. Groups are slow, we say, painful and frustrating. They make camels when they are out to design horses. You can't run a company by committee. Oh, God, not another meeting! Those complaints reflect some of the heavy costs of many group–committee–task force–type participative organizations—time costs and the hobbling of individual autonomy and experimentation. Such organizations demand frequent interaction that not only takes time but also requires the reporting of progress at frequent intervals. The older command-and-control models shackled individualism by chaining employees to their jobs with time clocks and short work cycles. Groupy organizations often frustrate individualism by forcing one to sit there endlessly trying to appreciate everybody else's point of view.

Pathfinding organizations, like all organizations, have to deal with group issues—if for no other reason than that groups will always be there. But groups also have certain characteristics that are quite consonant with pathfinding styles. For instance, small groups sometimes show high degrees of spontaneity. They can be both self-organizing and self-dissolving. They can come and go as their members need one another. Such spontaneous, temporary kinds of groups are quite in line with (and even necessary for) path-finding organizations. In such fluid, rapidly changing organizations, groups need not be formalized as permanent committees or boards. If some people feel that they need to work more closely together, they can either do it or seek the resources (including space and time) that will allow them to do it. And when they have done it, they can break up and re-form into other groups.

Pathfinding cultures, that is, need not throw out the baby with the bathwater. In their efforts to free up the individual, to mine imagination and entrepreneurship, they had better not kill off that second gold mine of energy and creativity, the small group. For what could be more enthusiastic, more creative, more motivating than a small gang of excited people bound closely together by their dedication to a hot idea?

Pathfinding organizations are likely to use small groups differently. They do much less prestructuring of such groups than do organizations aimed more at problem solving or implementing. Pathfinding cultures don't form many permanent groups. They don't cast particular groups in concrete or engrave them on organization charts. They tend, instead, to fertilize the garden, watch for new groups to sprout, nurture them with loving care, harvest the crop, and plant new seed.

Maintaining a pathfinding culture

Some of the special characteristics of pathfinding cultures turn out to be very hard to maintain over the long run. Pathfinding cultures value creativity, innovativeness, and determination in their members more than they value discipline or teamwork. Pathfinding cultures are flexible. They change rapidly. They are full of temporary groups that form and re-form as needed. They are governed by only a few laws. Their internal structures are loose and flat. They reward imaginativeness and championing behavior more than either solid workmanlike analysis or human warmth. And they reward effort as well as success.

Overall, such cultures thrive on excitement, change, constant reinvigoration. And those are, by definition, not steady state conditions. They are as distant as one possibly imagines from the green eyeshades and daily routines of many of our traditional organizations. They are always out of equilibrium. So they are hell to maintain.

All of us, at one time or another, have participated in challenging, urgent #1 pathfinding-type activities, but usually only for short spurts. We may have done it as kids when we were trying to build the hottest soapbox racer in the neighborhood or when we were inventing fund-raising schemes so that the band could get enough money to take that trip to Washington. While such experiences typically grow rarer as we grow older, most of us still engage in them once in a while, and we almost always value them as memorable: the researcher hot on the trail of something new, the do-it-yourselfer remodeling the kitchen, the author plugging away at the great novel, that exciting first trip abroad.

Unfortunately, such episodes are even rarer in most organizations than in our personal lives. Most of life in organizations is quite routine and predictable. In organizations, moreover, the very successes that such episodes spawn also sound their death knells. Once the job has been done, the excitement is gone. I remember a discussion with a group of engineers and scientists at Cal Tech's Jet Propulsion Lab some years ago: "Now that we know how to get a space shot to the moon," they said, "the fun is gone. From now on, it's just doing more of the same."

Pathfinding cultures try to keep such excitement and urgency going most of the time—not as a steady state but as a frequently recurring one. But maintaining such an atmosphere is very, very difficult. Both individuals and organizations are extremely adaptive. Today's excitement becomes tomorrow's normalcy. What's unusual this week is routine next week. After a while, most jobs come to require much more sweat than imagination.

How can an organization maintain excitement over long periods? No one knows for sure. Just as there are tricks that the clever host can use to jazz up the dying party, so too there are tricks for jazzing up the slowed-down organization: Feisty leaders can get on soapboxes and make inspirational speeches; or they can periodically kick people in the tail; or they can drag out some of the old gimmicks usually reserved for the last day of the annual sales meeting—loud music, prizes, and free trips to Bermuda. Some of those devices are helpful and appropriate, and imaginative companies can always think up new ones. But those devices can't come close to doing the whole job.

Probably the best long-run way to maintain a pathfinding culture is, paradoxically, by not working at it—at least not directly—but rather by fertilizing the well-seeded soil that enables and nurtures #1 behavior, whenever and wherever it may develop. Keeping a #1 culture going demands a kind of #1 faith—a faith like the farmer's faith that it is God and not the farmer who really grows the crops. The farmer only enables nature to do its miraculous work. The long-term maintainance of a #1 culture seems to require a faith like that. It requires a combination of leadership and organizational flexibility that *permits* more than it *causes* entrepreneurial, visionary excitement to sprout and grow. But this assumes that the organization has already made sure that the seed is the very best that can be found.

No organization, at this stage in history, can expect to achieve and maintain a high pathfinding plateau. Over time we must expect great variability in pathfinding cultures, high peaks and deep valleys. At some times, lots of hot items will be on the fire; then groups will spring up and new ideas will chain-react through the organization. At other times, things may be much more quiescent, even dull. The manager's job is to keep putting in the seed and to keep the soil warm and moist so that interesting new plants are always sprouting. If that isn't enough, he may have to go into a fertility dance.

Maintaining an ongoing pathfinding culture, that is, requires managers to show a curious combination of the tolerant faith of the farmer and the showmanship of the carnival barker.

That leaves us with a new (or is it an old?) paradox on our hands. If pathfinding leaders are typically passionate and visionary, and if the long-term maintenance of a whole organization's pathfinding style requires patience as well as push, then pathfinding leaders may not be ideal long-term guardians for pathfinding cultures.

As we suggested earlier, they often aren't. Strong, committed, impassioned leaders can stir up excitement in their organizations. By setting and preaching their clear and lucid missions, they can generate challenge and enthusiasm—as long as they are around. Indeed, sometimes they can't even do it for that long, especially in very large or fast-growing companies.

But institutionalizing such a pathfinding flavor, building it more or less permanently into the character of the organization, may require truly extraordinary forms of leadership, leadership dedicated to building just such organizations. Culture building may have to be the pathfinder's central mission.

It is from this special category of pathfinding leadership that ongoing pathfinding organizations are most likely to spring. A CEO mentioned earlier provides a good example. He was the one who had worked inside a huge and ponderous bureaucracy and came out of it with what he called an "ex-slave" mentality, dreaming of a free organization in which people could put their minds to work on interesting and important problems without all that Mickey Mouse stuff. He was dedicated to that kind of culture. Incidentally he was also dedicated to results. But he fought restrictions every step of the way. Leadership like his has a good chance of producing a fairly long-lived pathfinding culture, one that might continue to boil and bubble even after such a leader departs from the scene.

One more point: In the long run, the maintenance of such pathfinding cultures requires a good defense as well as a good offense. Pathfinding cultures are easily eroded by the predatory forces that typically surround them. Regulations can shackle them; cost controllers can nitpick them to death; lawyers can naysay them; boards of directors can starve them; and the press can jump all over them at the first sign of trouble. Just today, for example on June 1, 1985, as I write this, this Sunday morning's *San Jose Mercury News* (the major newspaper of California's Silicon Valley) ran a front page story on the reorganization of Apple Computer. Steve Jobs, the "eccentric" young leader and founder has been taken out of operating management. "In . . . three short months," the story reads, . . . "Apple Computer, Inc. has tumbled from being a flamboyant success to being a struggling and troubled computer company." In the same paper, on the same day, a table from *Datamation* lists Apple as number two after IBM with a 74 percent gain in revenues during the 1984 calendar year. Is Apple *really* in crisis? Is this the death knell of its culture? Has it *really* "tumbled"? Will the newspaper story help its prophecy to become self fulfilling? The management of meanings can be important! So one big piece of the job of maintaining a pathfinding culture is patrolling the dikes all through the long nights.

A reminder: Pathfinding cultures are risky

Going all out toward this wide-open pathfinding style can be very foolish. No one in a large organization, from the

CEO down, can ever be as free as the breeze. Human organizations, by their nature, constrain individual freedom.

A few years ago a thoughtful executive, lecturing to one of my MBA classes, shocked the students when he said something like this: "All organizations are prisons. The differences are that in some of them the cells are bigger and the food is better than in others." In large organizations, the movement, over the last three decades, from the classical #2 model toward a #3 participative model has undoubtedly helped enlarge the cells and improve the food. Movement to a full-scale #1 pathfinding model would give all the prisoners a full set of keys and reward them if they found ways to make number plates out of seaweed. Giving them the keys is the risky part. There's a fine line that differentiates organized anarchy from just plain anarchy. Pathfinding cultures need gutsy and determined leadership that is willing to take risks but is tempered by a little common sense too.

Movement toward a pathfinding culture also means some devolution of short-term power from the top downward. People at the top may then know less about what's going on, on a day-to-day basis. That can feel awfully frightening and dangerous (especially to lawyers). But it's scary for middle managers too, particularly in organizations where they may be summoned for detailed progress reports on a moment's notice. Moreover, in some segments of some companies, uniformity and standardized procedures may be so critical to quality and even survival that sensible managers will think long and hard before they ease off toward a looser pathfinding model.

For many reasons, managerial prudence is very much in order when the introduction of a pathfinding culture into a large and stable organization is being undertaken. The next (and last) chapter tries to put the pathfinding part of the managing picture back into its larger context. Managing, after all, involves more than just pathfinding.

Notes

[1] T. J. Peters and R. H. Waterman, *In Search of Excellence: Lessons from America's Best-Run Companies* (New York: Harper & Row, 1982).

[2] Quoted from *The Rule of St. Benedict*, trans. Abbot Justin McCann (Westminster, Md., 1952).

[3] F. J. Roethlisberger, *The Elusive Phenomena: An Autobiographical Account of My Work in the Field of Organizational Behavior at the Harvard Business School*. George F. F. Lombard, ed. (Boston: Division of Research, Harvard Business School, 1977), pp. 165–66.

10

KEEPING THE WHOLE ACT TOGETHER:
Pathfinding Is Only One Part of the Managing Process

While most of this book has argued for a revitalization of the pathfinding part of the managing process, it's time to put things back into a broader managerial context.

Passionate missionary #1 zeal deserves a significant place in each of us and in each of our organizations, but that ain't all there is! Visions of new worlds must be tempered by mundane realities like availability of resources, the state of technology, government regulations, lower-cost competition, tax laws, trade union contracts, and a thousand others. So it's time now to bring the #2 problem solving and #3 implementing actors back on center stage.

To do that, this last chapter aims at three related targets:

The first target is to see how we got here from there—to place our 1–2–3 model in historical perspective. How and why did pathfinding get lost in the shuffle in America while the other parts of the process, especially the #2 part, bounded ahead? Why did so many large Western companies forsake their heritage of entrepreneurial pathfinding?

The second target is to look at how American business schools, one major supplier of new managers, have dealt with the #1, #2, and #3 parts of the managing process. What have business schools really taught, and has it been the right stuff?

The third target is to consider how we can best get #1 back into the contemporary managerial scene. How can this be done in ways that will enrich both the practice of management and management education, and how can it be done without falling into the old trap of losing sight of the forest in our enthusiasm for one particular tree?

Getting here from there: The long 1–2–3 horse race

One can look at the last hundred years of managerial history as though it was one long three-horse race. The horses are, of course, called Pathfinder, Problem Solver, and Implementer. Since the race never ends, there are no final win, place, or show positions. But if we had taken a reading at any particular moment from, say, 1890 onward, we could get quite a clear fix on how each horse was doing at that instant. If we did that, we would find that it has been a curious race. The lead has changed about every 20 years.

Occasionally one of the three horses falls so far behind that its position seems utterly hopeless; but if we look again a decade later, that same animal somehow regained its vigor and is rapidly closing in on the other two.

In the beginning, before the turn of the century, the pathfinding horse had gotten off to a fine start. The churchmen, politicians, philosophers, and educators were all out there rooting for #1's individualistic, enterprising, do-it-yourself spirit. Even Abraham Lincoln, his memory still fresh at the end of the century, had said,

There is no permanent class of hired laborers among us. The prudent penniless beginner in the world labors for wages awhile, saves a surplus with which to buy tools or land for himself, then labors on his own account another while, and at length hires another new beginner to help him. . . . If any continue through life in the condition of the hired laborer, it is not the fault of the system, but because of either a dependent nature which prefers it, or improvidence, folly, or singular misfortune.[1]

But by 1910 or so the whole race had changed. Problem solving had begun to pull ahead, and pathfinding had begun to lag badly. The reason was the recent growth of the mass-production factory system. While the rugged independence of #1 was still being cheered onward by clerics and moralists, more pragmatic Americans were shifting their loyalties to the new #2 approach. The economic and productive power of the new factories was too great to ignore, even for moral reasons. This new analytic factory system, with its carefully planned systems and narrowly specialized jobs, could build good shoes without shoemakers, good guns without gunsmiths, in huge quantities and at low cost.

The arguments that these factories constituted a new form of slavery, "wage slavery," and were destroyers of individualism were easily rationalized. With swarms of uneducated immigrant workers arriving every day, one could (and did) argue that virtue, like beauty, was a matter of taste.

It was really virtuous and Christian to provide those poor souls with those repetitive factory jobs. So the economic power of the #2 model quickly pushed it far ahead, and it stayed ahead for the first couple of decades of the 1900s.

By the 1920s pathfinding had fallen far back. Economic growth and material productivity, not the old ethic of rugged individualism, were the order of the day. While patent applications dropped off, standardized model T's rattled off the Ford assembly lines by the thousands.

As for #3 implementing, it lagged along behind and in the service of #2. The #2 engineers planned it; then the #3 factory supervisors got their subordinates to do it—one way or another: by telling them or by selling them or by simply looking over every shoulder.

After World War II, the positions in the race changed again. In the 1950s both #2 and #3 took simultaneous great leaps forward. The arrival of the computer gave #2 a huge impetus. Operations researchers and systems analysts and computer scientists—all new arrivals—gave fresh and by now much-needed stimulation to old and tired #2 thinking. And #3 implementing, invigorated by the new human relations movement, finally showed a little muscle and began to gain on #2. As for #1, most of its supporters had long since quit the racecourse altogether, fanning out to freer roles as lawyers, shopkeepers, politicians, and academic researchers.

Organizations now began to grow fatter around their waists, adding engineers and analysts and middle managers at a great rate, while also growing thinner at their bottoms as the blue-collar era began to fade. Unlike their older brothers, the new analytic #2 types didn't carry stopwatches; they carried computers instead. They offered production scheduling methods and marketing models and linear programming solutions to raw materials mix problems. They began to dominate those fast-growing new American business schools, and thereby to control the supply of emerging new

MBAs. Thus energized, the new #2 horse raced ahead, a much more sophisticated beast than its predecessor, but still thinking in analytic, convergent ways.

In the 1950s, about the same time that #2 started getting its new look, #3 also got a big chance to make a move. By that time the bills piled up by the inequities of the old #2 approach had begun to come due. Trade union strength and worker alienation both increased. Things got so bad that a decade later Richard Nixon was proclaiming the decline of the American work ethic (and tending to blame it on soft educators). Companies were finding it much harder to make their hard-nosed old #2-type controls work as they used to. Troubles on the shop floor were coupled with even more troubles in coordinating and controlling all of those new technical and staff types that had begun to pour into the middle ranks of the company.

New ideas about "human relations" and "motivation" and "participation" gained some modest momentum in the 1950s. Unions initially rejected participative #3 notions as manipulative ploys, and managers saw them as threats to their prerogatives. So the #3 drive made its biggest gains by moving into the new middle-level white-collar and slide rule world where stopwatches and time clocks didn't have a chance. In that world, participative #3 types could make top management an offer it couldn't refuse: they could offer a way of controlling all those new knowledge workers. You can't get people like that to work effectively, the new voices argued, by narrowing their jobs or threatening to fire them for insubordination. The way to do it was the #3 way: make every one of them a member of the family. Involve people in planning; encourage small teams; go the participative route.

That was the new #3 line. And over the next decades—from the late 1950s up to the present—American managers very gradually began to accept it. Some managers adopted it consciously, and others slipped into it by inadvertence. The old analytic mentality slowly gave way to a softer, more human #3 style, but it happened mostly within the many levels of management itself. Managers began to talk more and more about improving communication, setting up task forces, motivating employees, and "getting along with people," and less and less about giving orders and maintaining management prerogatives.

So #2, which was now computerized, and #3, which was now participative, found new energy with which to surge forward into the 1960s, leaving #1 farther behind than ever. Indeed, it was as though #2 and #3, different as they were from each other, had formed a tenuous coalition to keep #1 from gaining ground. The #2 types despised those subjective, divergent, nonreasoning #1 styles of thinking; and #3s, with their commitment to power sharing and groupism, saw #1 types as authoritarian, paternalistic, dominating, and undemocratic.

In the 1960s and 70s, computer-carrying #2s ran the show and participative #3s maintained second place. By 1980, Japanese successes had helped catalyze American companies into more investment in #3 participative approaches, because such approaches were seen, at first, as the source of the high productivity of Japanese companies and the high quality of their products. So for a few years, from about 1980 to 1983, American management went through a painful period of self-assessment, reexamining its prior handling of #3 issues, especially vis-à-vis blue-collar manufacturing workers. The managers of Detroit's automobile companies had indeed done a lousy job on the #3 end. And they went to work to correct it.

In typically American fashion, and much more frenetically than in Europe, Americans debated, experimented, and sometimes ran around in circles—quality circles. That description is offered here with some chauvinistic pride, however, not with embarrassment. Americans respond quickly, often too quickly—but quickly. Critical books get written quickly and are quickly followed by books that offer quick solutions. Delegations quickly fly off to Japan; foundations quickly offer research grants; companies quickly give money to quickly formed new productivity centers. But that sound and fury does signify something—an active willingness to search for better ways.

Out of that search process has come, along with new #3-type experiments, a surprisingly unexpected resurgence of interest in the long-neglected #1 horse. Somebody finally noticed that he was still back there, lengths and lengths behind. Maybe if we could get him to move up a little, the whole race might become interesting again. Personal leadership again became a good phrase. So did such words as *mission, vision,* and *culture.* To improve the organization, the new #1 surge proposed, get some leaders in to lead it, simplify it, humanize it. Think less about systems and more about missions. Give your organization direction and purpose. Do it directly. Get out of your office, Mr. CEO. Get out there, and lead those foot soldiers as they charge up that hill. Fire the staff! They make things too complicated, and they distance you from your people.

As of this writing, that's how the horse race is going. Analytic #2s are out of favor and falling back. Operations researchers and management scientists are feeling defensive. They are rather silent, even on university campuses. Implementers are doing all right, and their products and services have evolved and changed. While humanism and participation are still around, it's the concept of *culture* that has given #3 its new energy. How long that will hold up is anybody's guess. And as #1 moves forward, there are signs of a search for a new coalition between individualistic mission-oriented #1 views and the new culture-oriented #3 views. Are they compatible? If they are, they may try to knock #2 thinking out of the race altogether. But that would be a destructive act, and no matter how hard they try, they won't succeed. It's only through the full participation of all three-horses that the whole race can be speeded up.

The end of the 2–3 model of management education: Managing requires more than just a sharp mind and a silver tongue

Business schools and their progeny, the MBAs, have grown and prospered enormously since about 1960. In that year 4,000 MBAs marched out of business schools. By 1980 the number had grown to about 60,000 annually. One reason was a major remodeling of management education helped by the Ford and Carnegie foundations. The new-style business school that emerged was aimed at teaching *numbers* and *people*. That #2–#3 combination made a lot of sense at the time because the new computer and new analytic tools promised valuable application to tough management problems. New work in the behavioral sciences also showed great promise for helping to solve tough human and organizational problems. So, with foundation money to back them up, the new business schools of the 60s went after #2 and #3 with a vengeance.

Paradoxically, even though #1 got left out in the cold, those were visionary #1 days in American business education. The #1 vision was of a new breed of very bright, analytically tooled-up young managers who would upgrade and professionalize American management.

In the most innovative business schools, like Carnegie Tech's Graduate School of Industrial Administration and MIT's Sloan School, both themes were implemented very well. Those schools went heavily into #2 by investing in the analytic disciplines of economics, statistics, math, and what later was called decision science. They also invested in the behavioral sciences to build up the #3 people side.

While managers out in the real world were initially reluctant about all of that number-crunching academic stuff, they soon got caught up in the new wave, and even reinforced it by bargaining up the price of the business school graduates. They did that to stay ahead of their competitors and also simply because those new kids were darn good. And the new kids got better every year as business schools gained status on their campuses. The new business schools provided a prescreened and selected labor pool for the fast-growing ranks of middle management. Starting salaries for MBAs climbed, and the cycle continued. More and better students applied to the business schools; the respectability of the schools rose; high-quality faculty became easier to recruit; and the content of business school courses evolved more and more toward the quantitative and the theoretical. The process fed on itself, and with all of those successes—in both the business and academic marketplaces—no one wanted to change the lineup.

The glamour companies got good press because they had the best and brightest analytic managers—McNamaras, Thorntons, Ashes. Consulting firms blossomed. The old consulting model, most often tied to work measurement and job analysis, gave way to strategic planning and organizational designing. The really hot consulting firms quickly learned to stay close to the major business schools and to attract many of their best students. The marriage was natural. The consultants gave primarily #2 kinds of advice, and the new MBAs knew more about #2 than about anything else. Indeed, the major clout of the new breed of MBAs has probably been delivered more through the consulting mechanism than through any other, a fact that may someday come to be seen as one of the tragic failings of American management education. When the organizations of our nation needed leaders, was it appropriate to offer them consultants?

Toward the end of the 1970s a few blemishes became

visible in the MBA image. That glamorous image began to look like the picture of Dorian Gray. Was this really a portrait of orderly intelligence and analytic competence? Or were shadows of arrogance, rigid insensitivity, and even amorality hiding there? The new professional MBA-type manager began to look more and more like the professional mercenary soldier—ready and willing to fight any war, and to do it coolly and systematically, without ever asking the tough #1 questions: Is this war worth fighting? Is it the right war? Is the cause just? Do I believe in it?

Some readers will recall that during the 60s and 70s many companies and many educators argued that a manager was a manager was a manager, that a well-trained manager could step into any business, pretty much any time. That view was proved wrong again and again. Remember GE's fiasco in France when it first acquired Machines Bull, the French computer company? GE sent over a good manager, but he knew no French, almost nothing about computers, and very little about French politics, French trade unions, or French culture. To put it mildly, things didn't work out very well.

When that optimistic belief that a good manager could manage anything began to crumble, we modified it to argue that a good manager also needed to know the particular business he was managing. But in the last few years many of us have found it necessary to modify that position even further. This time the addendum reads, "And for the long term, he or she had also better believe in that business."

So the submerged #1 part of the managing process has begun to reemerge in the practice of management. It is also showing small signs of reemerging in management education. American business schools are reassessing themselves. For the first time in 30 years, words like *leadership, power, entrepreneurship,* and *mission* have become respectable again.

But the incorporation of #1 materials into business

school courses is moving very slowly. Faculty members, like many middle managers, are very territorial. They tend to interpret any change anywhere in sight as a threat. So the implementation of #1 changes may be slowest where it should be fastest, in the leading business schools.

Toward a managerial trinity: Fitting #1 back into the managing process

Both managerial planning and implementing have, by default, often acted as the masters of purpose rather than its servants. That gets organizations into trouble. Without some overarching human purpose to steer by, even the best planning and the most skillful implementing can leave organizations spinning in endless circles. Whether for the whole organization or for the single manager, proactive vision, intent, and purpose anchor and prioritize the managing process.

Much of our recent thinking about managing has either ignored or denied the role of such #1 human intention. Yet without clear intention, a kind of uncertain other-directedness prevails. In marketing, for example, we have often used only market research results to decide what products and services to offer. We have argued reactively that our job is to give the consumer what the consumer wants. If the leaders of organizations take that idea too seriously, they find themselves without any proactive forward push. Their job becomes a passive-reactive one: Let's find out what they want and then give it to them. It's time, isn't it, to restore a little proactivity to the management mix.

In manufacturing, similarly, some of our companies have looked outward for panaceas to cure their malaises. They bought all of the fashionable gimmicks that consultants could think up. In the early 80s, in a particularly powerful spasm of reactivity, some of our organizations even started importing Oriental folk remedies. Those foreign bodies were immediately implanted under the skins of our unready organizations. Some of the remedies really helped, but even so they were often abandoned after a year or two in favor of newly touted cure-alls.

A little more looking inward is now in order, to give clearer purpose to our searches for answers. What are we trying to do here? Where are we trying to go? In the ill-defined field called strategic planning, some movement toward more inner-direction has already become visible. From the formula approach of the 1970s (If it's a cash cow, milk it!), strategists are more and more asking managers questions about intent and belief, as precursors to strategic plans.

Consider, further, how the inclusion of the #1 part of managing might enrich currently popular and useful contingency models of managing. Contingency theories make the sensible argument that there is no one best way. In some situations, leaders should firmly make unilateral decisions; in others, the "right" behavior is consultative, with the leader seeking advice or even consensus from subordinates. But the contingency models have typically been built without regard for #1 issues. These models define the "right way" as the #2–#3 reactive way. The rules run like this: First, conduct a #2 diagnosis of the situation. Then, if the situation has informational and other characteristics of type B or C, the manager should consult with subordinates before making a decision. But if the diagnosis indicates the situation to be of type D or E, let the manager make the decision by himself, and forthwith. And so on. First analyze, then act accordingly, just as the doctor does when you tell him about your stomachache.

What's wrong with that? It's certainly sensible to behave differently in different situations! What's wrong is that if managers take such rules seriously—no matter how sensible the rules—they give up their personhood. They do what the situation demands of them, not what they demand of the situation. If young managers follow such rules rigidly, they will manage a rudderless boat in a heavy sea.

Notice the dilemma here. On the first day of their training program, 50 student managers might offer 50 different answers when confronted with the same problem. But on the seventh day, if we teachers have done our jobs properly, shouldn't all 50 come up with the same answer to the same problem? Aren't there, in truth, better and worse ways to deal with management situations? And shouldn't we be teaching students the better ways? The contingent theorists make the case that that's what they're doing, teaching the better ways. And yet, because we hold #1 as well as #3 values, many of us bridle uncomfortably at the thought of having all managers handle the same situation in the same way.

But it is not such cookie cutter uniformity of behavior that should concern us. Far better uniformity than variations born of ignorance. It is the absence of individual purpose that should really worry us. If each of those young managers knew what he or she believed and wanted, their answers would not be uniform. The differences, however, would not result from ignorance, but from differing priorities. This young manager is out to develop his subordinates, so he discusses the problem with his people even when it is not strictly necessary; that one wants to communicate the mission she feels is vital, so she uses this particular situation as an instrument through which to get her larger message across; and so on. Like good sculptors, good managers should know how to handle the materials and tools of their trade; but that hardly means that all their sculptures must look alike. The individual creative visions of such managers will make sure of that, and will also keep innovation alive and well.

So there are riches to be mined by including the pathfinding factor in the management equation. For the organization, pathfinding leadership can provide stimulation, direction, and social control. For individual managers, at all organizational levels, attention to #1 adds mission and inspiration for oneself and for one's subordinates. Perhaps even more important, it adds a basis for setting priorities among the great number of problems that find the manager each day.

The pace of management will not slow down. It will continue to be frenetic, perhaps even more frenetic than in the past. Those quick exchanges in the corridor will continue, as will the perpetually full in-box, the incessant phone calls, and the emergency meetings. But with the #1 part of managing firmly in place inside the manager's head, the memos, phone calls, and meetings that really matter can be readily separated from those that don't. Forward movement can take place, even as we appear to be running in circles.

Managers can create the futures they want, but only if they understand what they want and if they want it very much.

A final caveat

While this book has extolled the virtues of the Pathfinding Church of Management, #1 dreams are not the only stuff that managing is made of.

In the past couple of years Western management has, in effect, decided for itself that it needs a kick in the tail, a rebirth of excitement. At this writing, it is beginning to do a pretty impressive job of self-renewal. But there's a danger—more than a danger, there is a high probability—that some organizations (including some business schools) will overreact, responding to all that criticism by throwing out all the old furniture and replacing it with chrome and plastic. This year ideas about mission and culture may look like the right furniture. But things don't really work that way. The books and articles, including this one, that urge personal leadership, vision, and charisma are probably right. Managers really ought to look more like those Civil War statues in the park—mounted on their great stallions, pointing the way. But charismatic leadership by itself just won't do it. We do need personal leadership and strong belief and clear purpose. We need earthy managers who get out there on the shop floor, smoking cigars with the lathe operators. But we also need those irritating MBA analysts and their little machines that talk in tongues. And we also need those silken-throated salesmen peddling their snake oil.

Pathfinding won't work by itself any more than good number crunching or skillful implementing will work by itself. We still need information and analysis and forecasts from the #2 part of the house, to tell us that it will cost too much, or that quality is falling off, or that Indonesian law won't allow us to sell it that way. And we still need some of the old-style hands-on #3 parts—incentives and career planning and sales promotions and all the rest.

But we also need pathfinding. Vision, values, and determination add soul to the organization. Without them, organizations react but do not create; they forecast but do not imagine; they analyze but do not question; they act but do not strive.

While pathfinding vision, values, and determination are not enough, we can't go very far without them.

Note

[1] Quoted in D. T. Rodgers, *The Work Ethic in Industrial America: 1850–1920* (Chicago: University of Chicago Press, 1974), p. 35.

INDEX